**MILITARY AVIATION LIBRARY**
**Modern**

European
# Aircraft

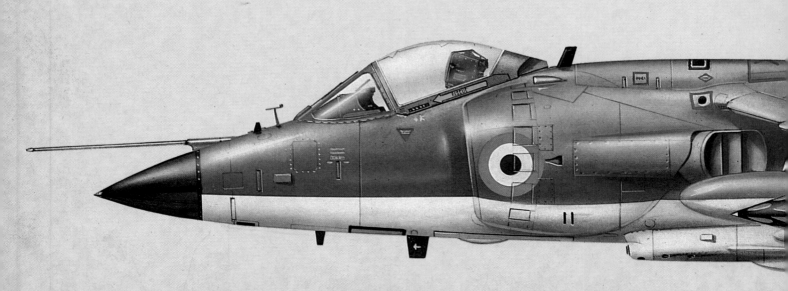

# MILITARY AVIATION LIBRARY
## Modern
# European Aircraft

**Bill Gunston**

CHARTWELL
BOOKS, INC.

Published by Chartwell Books Inc., New York

© Salamander Books Ltd., 1985

Colour profiles, cutaways and three-view drawings © Pilot Press Ltd.

ISBN: 0 89009 897 2

## PICTURE CREDITS

Aeritalia: 8.
Aero: 10.
Aerospatiale: 11.
Agusta: 14 (top).
BAe: 14, 15, 23 (top), 28, 42, 43, 44, 45.
Brazilian Air Force: 9 (bottom).
CASA: 30.
Dassault Breguet: 31, 33, 34, 35, 37, 38, 39 (top).
Dornier: 39 (bottom).
Flight International: 36, 54 (top).
Bill Gunston Collection: 60 (bottom right).
Industrial Photo Laboratories: 23 (bottom).
Martin/General Dynamics: 19.
MBB: 40.
McDonnell Douglas: 22 (bottom).
Panavia: 41.
Rolls-Royce 9 (top), 12, 13, 56 (top).
Saab-Scania: 46, 47, 49, 50.
Soko: 54 (bottom).
J. W. R. Taylor Collection: 55.
Transall: 56 (bottom).
UK Ministry of Defence: 17, 18, 22 (top), 24, 25, 26, 27, 29, 57, 61.
US Marine Corps: 21.
Westland: 58, 60 (left and top right).

# Contents

| | |
|---|---|
| Aeritalia G222 | **8** |
| Aermacchi M.B.326 and 329 | **9** |
| Aero L-29 Delfin | **10** |
| Aero L-39 Albatros | **10** |
| Aérospatiale Super Frelon | **11** |
| Aérospatiale/Westland Gazelle | **12** |
| Aérospatiale/Westland Puma and Super Puma | **13** |
| Agusta A109 Hirundo | **14** |
| BAe 748, Andover and Coastguarder | **14** |
| BAe Buccaneer | **15** |
| BAe Canberra and Martin/GD B-57 | **18** |
| BAe Harrier and Sea Harrier | **20** |
| BAe Hawk | **23** |

| | | | | |
|---|---|---|---|---|
| BAe Lightning | **24** | | MBB BO 105 | **40** |
| BAe Nimrod | **25** | | Panavia Tornado | **41** |
| BAe Strikemaster and 145 | **28** | | Saab 105 | **46** |
| BAe Victor | **29** | | Saab 35 Draken | **47** |
| CASA C-101 Aviojet | **30** | | Saab 37 Viggen | **48** |
| CASA C-212 Aviocar | **30** | | SEPECAT Jaguar | **51** |
| Dassault Breguet Atlantic | **31** | | SIAI-Marchetti SF.260 | **54** |
| Dassault Breguet Mirage F1 | **32** | | Soko Galeb and Jastreb | **54** |
| Dassault Breguet Mirage III and 5 | **34** | | Soko/CNIAR IAR 93 Orao | **55** |
| Dassault Breguet Mirage IVA | **36** | | Transall C-160 | **56** |
| Dassault Breguet Mirage 2000 | **37** | | Westland Scout and Wasp | **57** |
| Dassault Breguet Super Etendard | **38** | | Westland Sea King and Commando | **58** |
| Dassault Breguet/Dornier Alpha Jet | **39** | | Westland/Aérospatiale Lynx | **60** |

# Aeritalia G222

## G222

**Origin:** Aeritalia SpA, Naples (main factory Turin; new plant at Amendola, Naples, near corporate headquarters), Italy.
**Type:** Tactical transport.
**Engines:** Two 3,400shp General Electric T64-P4D single-shaft turboprops made under licence by Fiat; export option of two 6,100ehp Rolls-Royce Tyne 20, flat rated to 3,800ehp each.
**Dimensions:** Span 94ft 6in (28·8m); length 74ft 5½in (22·7m); height 32ft 1¾in (9·8m).
**Weights:** Empty 32,165lb (14,590kg); maximum useful load 19,840lb (9000kg); maximum loaded 58,422lb (26,500kg).
**Performance:** Maximum speed 336mph (540km/h) at 15,000ft; cruising speed 224mph (360km/h); initial climb 2,034ft (620m)/min; take-off or landing over 50ft (15m) about 2,700ft (825m); service ceiling 29,525ft (9000m); range with 11,025lb (5000kg) load 1,833 miles (2950km); ferry range 3,075 miles (4950km).
**Armament:** None.
**History:** First flight 18 July 1970; service delivery December 1975.
**Users:** Argentina, Dubai, Italy, Libya.

**Development:** In the early 1960s the NATO NBMR-4 competition had more than a dozen companies in Europe and North America sketching V/STOL transports with lift jets to meet the extremely short field-length requirement. None of these ever came to anything except the Fiat G222, with two Dart turboprops and eight lift jets. Eventually the lift jets were replaced by fuel, the Darts were replaced by T64 engines and despite an increase of two tonnes in empty weight the G222 eventually won an order for 12 aircraft placed in 1974. The Italian AF has a requirement for 44, and this number is expected to be built. Two more were ordered in 1974 by Argentina, with a third on option. This neat but rather limited machine can carry 44 troops, 32 paratroops, 36 stretchers (litters) plus eight attendants or sitting casualties, or various light trucks and artillery. Manufacture is shared by many Italian companies, and in an urgent need to win more orders demonstrations have been made in Egypt and Tunisia.

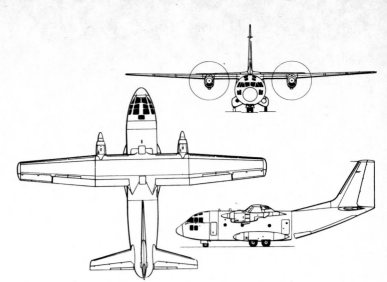

**Above: Three-view of G222 production aircraft.**

In 1979 production was starting on 20 G222L for Libya, powered by the Tyne 20 (the USA having refused export rights for the T64). This much more powerful version is expected to become a standard export option.

**Below: Italian paratroops leave in a stick from one of the first G222s now joining the Aeronautica Militare Italiano.**

**Above: G222 of Aeronautica Militare Italiano.**

# Aermacchi M.B. 326 and 339

## M.B.326 and 326 GB and GC (AT-26 Xavante), 326K (Atlas Impala), 326L and M.B.339

**Origin:** Aeronautica Macchi SpA (Aermacchi); licence-production in Australia, Brazil and S Africa.

**Type:** Two-seat basic trainer and light attack aircraft; (326K) single-seat trainer/attack; (339) two-seat all-through trainer.

**Engine:** One Rolls-Royce Viper single-shaft turbojet; (original production versions) 2,500lb (1134kg) thrust Viper 11; (GB, GC, H and M) 3,410lb (1547kg) Viper 20 Mk 540; (K, L and 339) 4,000lb (1814kg) R-R/Fiat Viper 632-43.

**Dimensions:** Span (over tip tanks) 35ft 7in (10·85m); length 34ft 11in (10·64m); height 12ft 2½in (3·72m).

**Weights:** Empty (G trainer) 5,920lb (2685kg); (G attack) 5,640lb (2558kg); (K) 6,240lb (2830kg); maximum loaded (G trainer) 10,090lb (4577kg); (G attack) 11,500lb (5217kg); (K and 339) 12,500lb (5670kg).

**Performance:** Maximum speed (G clean) 539mph (867km/h); (K clean) 553mph (890km/h); (339) 560mph (901km/h); initial climb (G clean) 6,050ft (1844m)/min; (G attack at max wt) 3,100ft (945m)/min; (K clean and 339) 6,500ft (1980m)/min; service ceiling (G trainer clean) 47,000ft (14,325m); (G attack, max wt) 35,000ft (10,700m); range on internal fuel (G trainer) 1,150 miles (1850km); (K with max weapons) about 160 miles (260km).

**Armament:** Six underwing pylons for load of up to 4,000lb (1814kg) including bombs, rockets, tanks, missiles, reconnaissance pods or gun pods; some versions have single 7·62mm or similar gun (or Minigun) in fuselage; 326K (Impala) has two 30mm DEFA 553 cannon in fuselage, each with 125 rounds. (339) two 30mm DEFA cannon can be carried in wing-mounted slipper pods; other options as 326.

**History:** First flight 10 December 1957; (production 326) 5 October 1960; (K prototype) 22 August 1970; (339) 12 August 1976.

**Users:** Argentina, Australia, Bolivia (X), Brazil (X), Dubai, Ghana, Italy, S Africa, Togo (X), Tunisia, Zaire, Zambia, Zimbabwe-Rhodesia (Atlas). X = Xavante.

**Development:** The most successful Italian military aircraft programme in history, the 326 was designed by a team led by Ermanno Bazzocchi and was put into production as a trainer for the Regia Aeronautica, which received 90. In addition the South African AF has over 150 K models, built by Atlas Aircraft with locally built engines, and expects to build over 200, while other big customers include Australia (114, 85 built by CAC in Melbourne), Brazil (122 locally built Xavantes) and many emergent nations. The latest sub-types are the 326K with the most powerful Viper, the 326L with two seats but K attack capability, the M uncompromised dual trainer and the M.B. 339 with redesigned airframe for all-through training, with raised instructor seat under a sloping canopy. Despite having a largely redesigned structure the 339 is hoped (optimistically) to be priced at only £850,000.

**Above: First prototype M.B.339, a completely redesigned aircraft with modern stepped cockpits. Aermacchi hope to sell to many air forces by being cheaper than the opposition.**

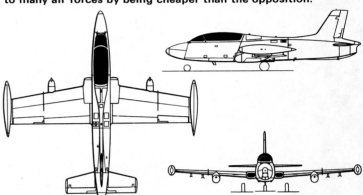

**Above: Three-view of typical M.B.326G with wing gun pods.**

**Below: The EMBRAER AT-26 Xavante of the Brazilian Air Force is the M.B.326GB built under licence. By spring 1977 over 120 had been delivered to attack, recce and training units.**

# Aero L-29 Delfin

## L-29 Delfin (NATO name "Maya")

**Origin:** Aero Vodochody national corporation, Czechoslovakia.
**Type:** Basic trainer.
**Engine:** One 1,960lb (890kg) thrust M-701 single-shaft turbojet.
**Dimensions:** Span 33ft 9in (10.29m); length 35ft 5½in (10.81m); height 10ft 3in (3.13m).
**Weights:** Empty 5,027lb (2280kg); maximum loaded 7,804lb (3540kg).
**Performance:** Maximum speed at 16,400ft (5000m) 407mph (655km/h); initial climb 2,755ft (840m)/min; service ceiling 36,090ft (11,000m); maximum range on internal fuel 397 miles (640km).
**Armament:** Two wing hardpoints on which can be attached two 7.62mm guns, small tanks, or various other loads including bombs of up to 220lb (100kg).
**History:** First flight 5 April 1959; service delivery 1963; final delivery 1974.
**Users:** Bulgaria, Czechoslovakia, Egypt, E Germany, Guinea, Hungary, Indonesia, Iraq, Nigeria, Romania, Soviet Union, Syria, Uganda.

**Development:** Designed by a team led by K. Tomas and the late Z. Rublic, the L-29 was Czecholsovakia's submission in 1960 as the standard Warsaw

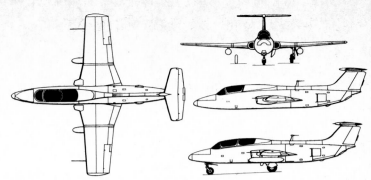

**Above: Three-view of L-29 (plus side view of L-29A Akrobat single-seat version for aerobatic demonstration).**

Pact trainer. It won, and though disgruntled Poland went ahead with the TS-11 Iskra, other Communist countries and several other air forces adopted this trainer and more than 3,000 were delivered. Two variants, not built in quantity, were the L-29A single-seat aerobatic version and the L-29R for counter-insurgency operations with nose cameras and under-wing stores.

# Aero L-39 Albatros

## L-39, L-39Z

**Origin:** Aero Vodochody national corporation, Czechoslovakia.
**Type:** Basic and advanced trainer.
**Engine:** One 3,792 (1720kg) thrust Walter Titan two-shaft turbofan (licence-built Ivchenko AI-25-TL).
**Dimensions:** Span 31ft 0½in (9.46m); length 40ft 5in (12.32m); height 15ft 5½in (4.72m).
**Weights:** Empty 7,341lb (3330kg); maximum loaded 10,141lb (4600kg).
**Performance:** Maximum speed at 16,400ft (5000m) 466mph (750km/h); Mach limit in dive 0.80; cruising speed at 5000m, up to 423mph (700km/h); initial climb 4,330ft (1320m)/min; service ceiling 37,075ft (11,300m); max range at 5000m on internal fuel 565 miles (910km).
**Armament:** Provision for light external load of tanks, bombs, rockets or 7.62mm gun pods (weight unstated) on two hardpoints under wings; internal fittings confined to gun-camera and sight.
**History:** First flight 4 November 1968; service delivery late 1973.
**Users:** Afghanistan, Czechoslovakia, Iraq, Soviet Union (probably other Warsaw Pact in due course).

**Development:** Designed by a team led by Jan Vlcek, the L-39 is succeeding well in its task of replacing the L-29, and in 1972 it was accepted in principle as the future trainer of all Warsaw Pact countries except Poland. It forms

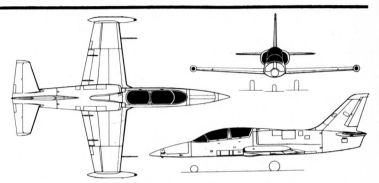

**Above: Three-view of L-39 Albatros.**

part of an integrated pilot-training system which includes a flight simulator, ejection-seat trainer and mobile automatic test equipment. The L-39Z was under development in 1973 as a light attack version which, like all L-39s, can be operated from unpaved surfaces. Iraq is believed to have ordered both models.

**Below: The shapely turbofan-powered Albatros marks a great advance over the mass-produced Delfin. It will be interesting to see how well it does in the world trainer market.**

# Aérospatiale Super Frelon

## 321 G, Ja and L

**Origin:** Soc. Aérospatiale, France.

**Type:** (G) Anti-submarine and offshore patrol helicopter; (Ja, L) utility transport.

**Engines:** Three 1,630hp Turboméca Turmo IIIC turboshafts.

**Dimensions:** Diameter of main (six-blade) rotor 62ft (18·9m); length (rotors turning) 75ft 7in (23m); height (tail rotor turning) 21ft 10in (6·66m).

**Weights:** Empty, equipped 14,607lb (6626kg); maximum 28,660lb (13,000kg).

**Performance:** Maximum speed 171mph (275km/h) (a Super Frelon prototype in racing trim set a record at 212mph in 1963); maximum rate of climb 1,312ft (400m)/min (three engines), 479ft (146m)/min (two engines); service ceiling 10,325ft (3150m); endurance in ASW role 4hr.

**Armament:** See text.

**History:** First flight, SA.3210 Super Frelon December 1962; SA 321G November 1965.

**Users:** China, France (Aéronavale), Iran, Israel, Libya, S. Africa; Syria reported but unconfirmed by Aérospatiale.

**Development:** The biggest and heaviest helicopter yet produced in quantity to a West European design, the Super Frelon first flew in 1962 at the Marignane (Marseilles) plant of what was then Sud-Aviation. It was derived from the SA.3200 Frelon with the assistance of Sikorsky Aircraft whose technology and experience were used in the lifting and tail rotors and drive systems. Fiat of Italy assisted with the main gearbox and power transmission and continue to make these parts. The Super Frelon has been made in three versions: SA 321F civil airliner; SA 321G anti-submarine and SA 321Ja utility. The 321Ja is the most numerous version and has been sold to several air forces. A sub-variant called SA 321L serves in quantity with the South African Air Force, and Israel used Super Frelons to carry commando raiders to Beirut Airport. The 321G is a specialised ASW aircraft, which equips Flotille 32F of the Aéronavale (French Naval Air Arm). It operates in groups, usually of four, one carrying a Sylphe panoramic radar and dunking sonar to find targets and the others each armed with four homing torpedoes. In the anti-ship role the 321G can carry two of the big Exocet long-range missiles. Another role is towing and mine-sweeping

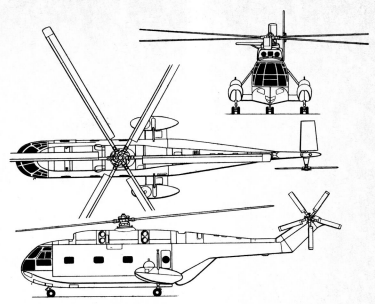

**Above: Three-view of SA 321Ja (most non-radar versions similar).**

and the three powerful engines provide enough power reserve for a towing pull of 6,600lb (3000kg). All combat Super Frelons can operate from airfields, ships or from water.

**Below: Though the primary mission of most of the SA 321G Super Frelon force of the Aéronavale is anti-submarine patrol in support of the French nuclear-missile submarines, this G-model is seen engaged in launch tests for the AM39 Exocet missile. Weighing 1,430lb (650kg), the air-launched version of Exocet is a formidable anti-ship missile, with speed of Mach 0·93 and range (helicopter-launched at 330ft altitude) of just over 32 miles (52km).**

# Aérospatiale/Westland Gazelle

## SA 341B, C, D, E, F and H and SA 342K

**Origin:** Aérospatiale, Marignane, France; produced in association with Westland Helicopters, Yeovil, UK; licence-produced by Soko, Yugoslavia.
**Type:** Multi-role utility helicopter.
**Engine:** One 592shp Turboméca Astazou turboshaft (IIIA, IIIC or IIIN, depending on customer); (SA 342K) 858shp Astazou XIVH flat-rated at 592shp.
**Dimensions:** Diameter of three-blade main rotor 34ft 5½in (10·50m); length overall (rotors turning) 39ft 3¼in (11·97m); height 10ft 2½in (3·15m).
**Weights:** Empty (H) 2,002lb (908kg); maximum loaded (H) 3,970lb (1800kg), (342J) 4,190lb (1900kg).
**Performance:** Maximum cruise 164mph (264km/h); range with max fuel 416 miles (670km), (with 1,102lb/500kg payload) 223 miles (360km).
**Armament:** Two pods of 36mm rockets, two forward-firing Miniguns or four AS.11, Hot or TOW misslies or two AS.12, each with appropriate sight system, side-firing Minigun, GPMG or Emerson TAT with sight system.
**History:** First flight 7 April 1967, (production 341) 6 August 1971.
**Users:** (Military) include Egypt, France, Kuwait, Qatar, Senegal, UK (Army, RAF, RN), and Yugoslavia.

**Development:** A natural successor to the Alouette, this trim five-seater has much higher performance, and has been cleared for IFR Cat.I operation. Orders placed under the Anglo-French agreement of February 1967—which made this French design a joint project—included 135 Gazelle AH.1 (341B) for the British Army, and smaller numbers of HT.2 (341C)

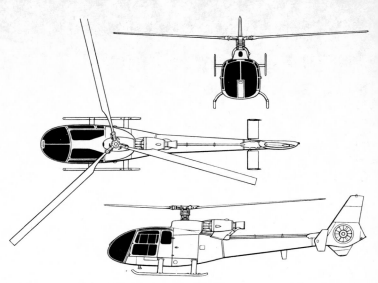

**Above: Three-view of typical SA 341 with Astazou IIIA, no wheels.**

for the Navy and HT.3 and HCC.4 (D and E) for the RAF. The 341F is the French Army type, the H the export variant and the 342K the first of a heavier and basically more powerful family. By 1980 Aérospatiale was also delivering the bigger Dauphin.

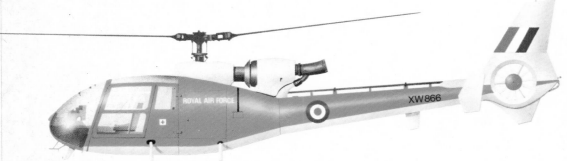

**Above: Gazelle HT.3 trainer of RAF CFS, Shawbury.**

**Below: Today the Alouette is vulnerable over the battlefield, but the much faster and more nimble Gazelle has a fair chance of survival. This Gazelle AH.1 of the British Army is scouting on manoeuvres with armour (the Chieftain Mk 3 battle tank has its turret pointing astern). Note the two blade aerials under the tail boom for Army communications.**

# Aérospatiale/Westland
# Puma and Super Puma

## SA 330B, C, E, H and L and SA 331 Super Puma

**Origin:** Aérospatiale, Marignane, France; produced (except 331) in association with Westland Helicopters, Yeovil, UK.

**Type:** All-weather transport.

**Engines:** (330) two Turboméca Turmo turboshaft, (B, C, E) 1,328hp Turmo IIIC4, (H, L) 1,575hp Turmo IVC; (331) two 1,800hp Turboméca Makila.

**Dimensions:** Diameter of four-blade main rotor 49ft 2½in (15·00m); length overall (rotors turning) 59ft 6½in (18·15m), (331) over 67ft (20m); height 16ft 10½in (5·14m).

**Weights:** Empty (H) 7,795lb; maximum loaded (H) 15,430lb (7000kg), (L) 16,315lb (7400kg), (331) about 22,050lb (10,000kg).

**Performance:** Maximum cruise (S/L) 159mph (257km/h); max range with standard fuel (330, typical) 360 miles (580km).

**Armament:** Many customer options including weapon pylons for gun pods or missiles, and various axial- or side-firing cannon or Minigun installations.

**History:** First flight 15 April 1965; service delivery (330B) April 1969.

**Users:** (Military) includes Abu Dhabi, Algeria, Belgium, Cameroun, Chad, Chile, Ecuador, France, Gabon, Ivory Coast, Kuwait, Morocco, Nepal, Nigeria, Pakistan, Portugal, S Africa, Togo, Tunisia, UK (RAF), Zaïre.

**Development:** Developed for the French Army ALAT (Aviation Légèr de l'Armée de Terre), this fast and capable helicopter has surpassed all expecta-

**Three-view of SA 330 Puma, without armament.**

tions in sales to both military and civil customers. By 1977 sales exceeded 500, most of them outside the Anglo-French partner countries that build the original version. There are large sliding doors on each side and loads include 20 troops or 6,600lb (3000kg) slung. The technically more advanced Super Puma, likely to prove an equally successful machine, is not a collaborative project.

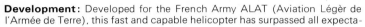

**Above: Puma HC.1 of 230 Sqn, RAF Odiham.**

**Below: Winching down a heavy load of goodies to some very exposed infantry from an even more exposed Puma HC.1 of 33 Sqn, in the RAF tactical helicopter force based at Odiham. Though designed to meet the needs of the ALAT (French Army Aviation), the Puma has proved to be exactly right for military customers (and now offshore oil support operators) all over the world. SA 331 Super Puma promises to be as great a sales success in the 1980s.**

# Agusta A109 Hirundo

## A 109A military and A 129 Mangusta

**Origin:** C. A. Giovanni Agusta, Gallarate, Italy.
**Type:** (A 109) multi-role, (129) gunship.
**Engines:** Two 420shp Allison 250-C20B turboshafts; (129) see text.
**Dimensions:** Diameter of four-blade main rotor 36ft 1in (11·00m); length overall (rotors turning) 42ft 10in (13·05m); height 10ft 10in (3·30m).
**Weights:** Empty about 3,120lb (1415kg); maximum loaded over 5,400lb (2450kg).
**Performance:** maximum cruise 165mph (266km/h); max range at S/L 351 miles (565km).
**Armament:** (109) one remotely sighted and aimed Minigun or GPMG and either two rocket pods or four TOW or Hot missiles with sight system.
**History:** First flight 4 August 1971; (production) 1976.
**Users:** Italian Army (evaluation).

**Development:** Not yet in production, the military version of the sleek and attractive A 109 is one of the smallest high-performance twin-turbine helicopters with all-weather capability. Five are being tried in simulated battle conditions by the Italian Army, primarily in the anti-tank role but also

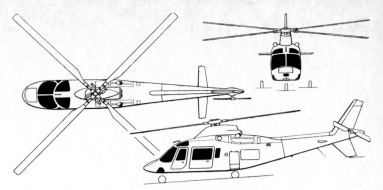

Above: Three-view of A 109A (without TOW missiles).

as electronic-warfare platforms, as troop carriers (seven plus pilot) and as casevac ambulances with two stretchers and two attendants. The projected A 129 would have a slim tandem-seat nose similar to that of the Hughes AH-64, with pilot in the rear, and extensive weapon options; proposed engines are Allison 250-C30 derated to 450hp, with 550hp available from either in emergency. The first of three should fly in 1981.

# BAe 748, Andover and Coastguarder

## HS.748, Andover, Coastguarder

**Origin:** Hawker Siddeley Aviation, Manchester, UK (also assembled by Hindustan Aeronautics, India).
**Type:** Multi-role transport; Coastguarder, maritime patrol.
**Engines:** Two 2,280ehp (2,140shp) Rolls-Royce Dart 534-2 or 535-2 single-shaft turboprops; (Andover C.1, two 3,245ehp Dart 201).
**Dimensions:** Span 98ft 6in (30·02m) (Andover C.1, 98ft 3in); length 67ft 0in (20·42m) (Andover C.1, 78ft 0in, 23·77m); height 24ft 10in (7·57m) (Andover C.1, 30ft 1in).
**Weights:** Empty (passenger) 27,000lb (12,247kg), (military freight) 25,516lb (11,574kg), (Coastguarder) about 27,000lb; maximum loaded 46,500lb (21,092kg) (Andover C.1, 50,000lb, 22,680kg; military overload limit 51,000lb, 23,133kg).
**Performance:** Typical cruise at 38,000lb, 281mph (452km/h); initial climb at 38,000lb, 1,420ft (433m)/min; typical military field length at normal gross weight 3,200ft (1000m); range with 20 per cent reserves at normal weight, 1,105 miles (1778km) with max load, 1,646 miles (2649km) with max fuel; radius of action at normal weight with airdrop of 12 containers of 750lb (340kg) 720 miles (1158km); (Coastguarder has almost doubled range and endurance).
**Armament:** Normally none, but options available on Coastguarder.
**History:** First flight 24 June 1960; (production Andover C.1) 9 July 1965; (Coastguarder) early 1977.
**Users:** (Military only) Argentina, Australia, Belgium, Brazil, Brunei, Cameroun, Colombia, Ecuador, Egypt, India, S Korea, Malaysia, Nepal, New Zealand, Tanzania, Thailand, UK (RAF, Royal Flight), Venezuela, Upper Volta, Zambia.

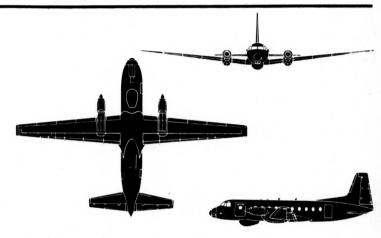

Above: Three-view of the HS.748 Coastguarder.

**Development:** Of total sales approaching 350, almost half of all versions of this versatile STOL transport have been military. The Andover C.1 is a redesigned aircraft with different wing, more powerful engines driving larger propellers, different fuselage with rear loading/dropping door, different tail and "kneeling" landing gear; the RAF uses 21 while 10 sold to New Zealand may later be equipped for maritime patrol. The latter is the primary duty of the Coastguarder, which has extra fuel, MAREC search radar, Decca Doppler/TANS computer and Omega VLF navigation, chute for flares and rescue dinghies sufficient for an entire 747-load of passengers. All military 748s have the option of a large freight door, strong floor and fittings for many specialized roles.

Left: The HS.748 is one of the mainstays of the Brazilian Air Force. The last six delivered have large freight doors of the kind pictured below.

Below: This Belgian 748 is fitted with a large rear freight door. The basically similar but much more powerful Andover C.1 is the only 748 version with a rear ramp door.

# BAe Buccaneer

## Buccaneer S.1, 2, 2A, 2B, 2C, 2D and 50

**Origin:** Hawker Siddeley Aviation (formerly Blackburn Aircraft, now British Aerospace), UK.
**Type:** Two-seat attack and reconnaissance.
**Engines:** (S.1) two 7,100lb (3220kg) thrust Bristol Siddeley (previously de Havilland) Gyron Junior 101 single-shaft turbojets; (all later marks) two 11,030lb (5003kg) Rolls-Royce Spey 101 two-shaft turbofans.
**Dimensions:** Span (1) 42ft 4in (12·9m); (2 and subsequent) 44ft (13·41m); length 63ft 5in (19·33m); height 16ft 3in (4·95m).
**Weights:** Empty (1) 26,000lb (2) about 30,000lb (13,610kg); maximum loaded (1) 46,000lb (20,865kg); (2) 62,000lb (28,123kg).
**Performance:** Maximum speed (all) 645mph (1038km/h, Mach 0·85) at sea level; initial climb (2, at 46,000lb) 7,000ft (2134m)/min; service ceiling not disclosed but over 40,000ft (9144m); range on typical hi-lo-hi strike mission with weapon load (2) 2,300 miles (3700km).
**Armament:** Rotating bomb door carries four 1,000lb (454kg) bombs or multi-sensor reconnaissance pack or 440gal tank; (S.2 and later) four wing pylons each stressed to 3,000lb (1361kg), compatible with very wide range of guided and/or free-fall missiles. Total internal and external stores load 16,000lb (7257kg).
**History:** First flight (NA.39) 30 April 1958; (production S.1) 23 January 1962; (prototype S.2) 17 May 1963; (production S.2) 5 June 1964; final delivery late 1975.
**Users:** S Africa, UK (RAF, Royal Navy).

**Above:** Spin-stabilized 68mm rockets ripple from the 18-tube launchers of a Buccaneer of the RAF.

**Below:** Buccaneer S.2 of 809 Sqn, Royal Navy, with flight-refuelling "Buddy" Mk 20B hose-reel pod on inner right pylon.

**Foot of page:** Low-level run by a Buccaneer S.2A of 12 Sqn, RAF. Over the years the Buccaneer has been equipped with ever-better ECM and other defensive avionics, some of which show externally. Most aircraft carry wing drop tanks and a fixed FR probe.

**▶Development:** After the notorious "Defence White Paper" of April 1957, which proclaimed manned combat aircraft obsolete, the Blackburn B.103, built to meet the naval attack specification NA.39, was the only new British military aircraft that was not cancelled. Development was grudgingly permitted, and this modest-sized subsonic machine was gradually recognised as a world-beater. Designed for carrier operation, its wing and tail were dramatically reduced in size as a result of very powerful tip-to-tip supercirculation (BLC, boundary-layer control) achieved by blasting hot compressed air bled from the engines from narrow slits. The S.1 (strike Mk 1) was marginal on power, but the greatly improved S.2 was a reliable and formidable aircraft. The first 84 were ordered by the Royal Navy and most of these have been transferred to RAF Strike Command, designated S.2B when converted to 'launch Martel missiles. Those remaining with the Navy are S.2Ds (2C if they are not Martel-compatible). In January 1963 the South African Air Force bought 16 S.50s with BS.605 boost rocket built into a retractable pack in the rear fuselage to facilitate use from hot and high airstrips. Finally — perhaps rather surprisingly, considering the scorn vented on Buccaneer during the TSR.2 era — the RAF signed in 1968 for 43 new S.2Bs with adequate equipment, including a refuelling probe which is never used in front-line service in Germany. Within the limits of crippling budgets the RAF Buccaneers have been updated by improved avionics and ECM, and all models have the advantage of an unbreakable long-life airframe and the ability to carry weapons internally. In 1977 they were getting Pave Spike laser-guided bomb systems. Altogether the Mk 2 Buccaneer is one of the most cost/effective aircraft ever designed for tactical use.

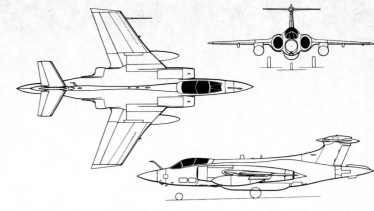

**Three-view of Buccaneer S.2 with FR probe and bomb-door tank.**

**Right:** One of the missions of the Buccaneer is the LABS "over the shoulder" toss of nuclear weapons. Here, in vertical attitude, is an S.2A of 16 Sqn.

**Far right:** Heading into the sunset, this S.2B of 15 Sqn, RAF Laarbruch, has bulged weapon-door fuel tank and rocket pods.

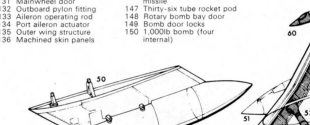

**Buccaneer S.2B of 16 Sqn, Laarbruch.**

1 In-flight refuelling probe
2 Radar scanner
3 Multi-mode search and fire-control radar
4 Weapon recorder
5 Radome (folded)
6 Radome hinge
7 Weapon release computer
8 Windscreen rain dispersal duct
9 Windscreen wiper
10 Birdproof windscreen
11 Pilot's head-up display
12 Instrument panel shroud
13 Rudder pedals
14 Nosewheel leg hinge point
15 Landing and taxi lamp
16 Shock absorber strut
17 Nosewheel forks
18 Aft retracting nosewheel
19 Avionics equipment
20 Engine throttles
21 Canopy side rail
22 Pilot's ejector seat
23 Seat firing handle
24 Aft sliding canopy
25 Observer's blast shield
26 Observer's instrument display
27 Starboard engine air intake
28 Observer's ejection seat
29 Cockpit floor structure
30 Head-up display symbol generator
31 Port engine air intake
32 Anti-icing air line
33 Air intake duct
34 Cockpit aft pressure bulkhead
35 Forward main fuselage fuel tank
36 Canopy motor
37 Canopy top rail
38 Rolls-Royce RB.168-1A Spey Mk 101 turbofan
39 Bleed air ducting
40 Detachable bottom cowling
41 Engine front mounting
42 Firewall frame
43 Engine aft mounting
44 Forward fuselage structure
45 Bleed air cross-over duct
46 Canopy hand winding shuttle
47 Detachable engine top cowling

48 Starboard slipper tank
49 Data link acquisition pod
50 Data link inboard pylon
51 Martel air-to-surface missile
52 Wing fold hinge line
53 Leading edge blowing air duct
54 UHF antenna
55 Dorsal spine structure
56 Anti-collision light
57 Wing-fold actuator
58 Wing-fold operating link
59 Starboard outer pylon
60 ARI 18218 aerial housing
61 Blown leading edge
62 Starboard navigation light
63 Formation light
64 Starboard blown aileron
65 Aileron actuator
66 Starboard wingtip (folded)
67 Aileron and flap blowing ducts
68 Starboard blown flap
69 Port wing tip (folded)
70 Centre fuselage fuel tank
71 Machined spar ring frames
72 Ring frame bolted attachment
73 Aft fuselage fuel tank
74 Electrical cable ducting in dorsal spine
75 Avionics equipment bay
76 Air data computer
77 HF notch aerial
78 Equipment bay cooling air intake
79 Fin spar attachment
80 Fin structure
81 Tailplane actuator
82 Tailplane operating rod
83 Tailplane blowing air duct
84 Bullet fairing
85 Forward passive warning system antenna
86 Blown tailplane leading edge
87 All-moving tailplane structure

88 Tailplane flap
89 Tailplane flap actuator
90 Hinge attachment point
91 Top fairing
92 Rear navigation light
93 Formation light
94 Aft passive warning system antenna
95 Port tailplane flap
96 Rudder structure
97 Rudder operating link
98 Rudder actuator
99 Airbrake jack
100 Drag-link hinge attachment
101 Airbrake operating slide
102 Split tailcone airbrake
103 Top strake
104 Honeycomb reinforcing panel
105 Bottom strake
106 Airbrake (open)
107 Hinge arm
108 Aft fuselage structure
109 Vent pipe
110 Arresting hook
111 Jet efflux fairing
112 Engine jet pipe
113 Bomb bay door actuator
114 Bomb door aft hinge
115 Port blown flap structure
116 Flap actuator
117 Port blown aileron
118 Blowing air duct
119 Wing spar bolted attachment
120 Wing fold actuator
121 Top of main undercarriage leg
122 Mainwheel well

123 Main undercarriage jack
124 Inboard blown leading edge
125 Inboard pylon fitting
126 430 Imp gal (1956 l) slipper tank
127 Wing fold main-spar hinge
128 Rear spar hinge
129 Main undercarriage levered suspension
130 Inboard retracting mainwheel
131 Mainwheel door
132 Outboard pylon fitting
133 Aileron operating rod
134 Port aileron actuator
135 Outer wing structure
136 Machined skin panels

137 Port wingtip
138 Formation light
139 Crash trip switches
140 Wing lifting lug
141 Port navigation light
142 Blown outboard leading edge
143 Pitot head
144 Port ARI 18218 aerial housing
145 Outboard pylon
146 Port Martel air-to-surface missile
147 Thirty-six tube rocket pod
148 Rotary bomb bay door
149 Bomb door locks
150 1,000lb bomb (four internal)

151 Forward hinge point
152 425 Imp gal (1932 l) bomb door auxiliary tank

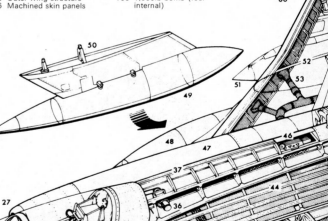

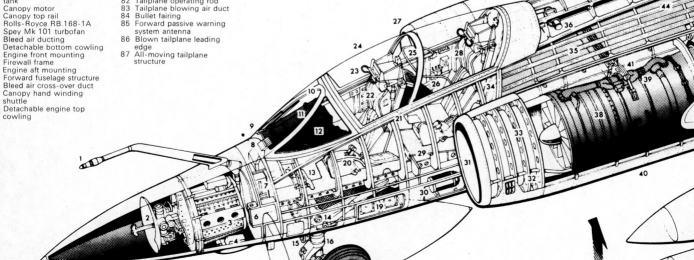

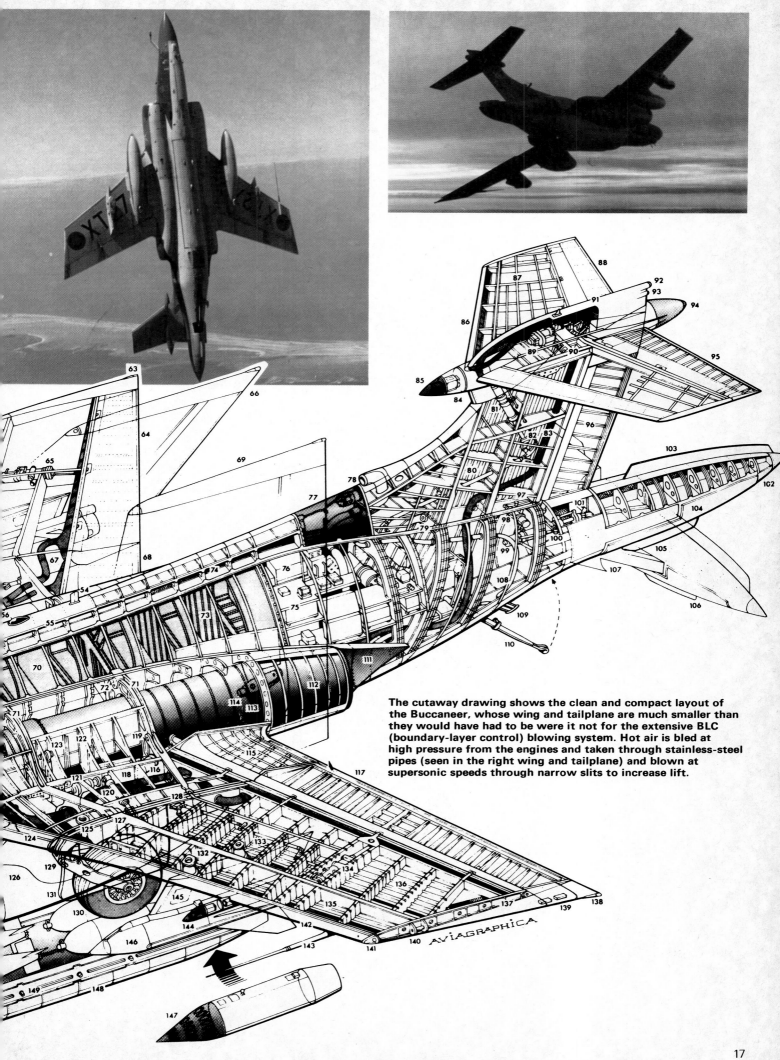

The cutaway drawing shows the clean and compact layout of the Buccaneer, whose wing and tailplane are much smaller than they would have had to be were it not for the extensive BLC (boundary-layer control) blowing system. Hot air is bled at high pressure from the engines and taken through stainless-steel pipes (seen in the right wing and tailplane) and blown at supersonic speeds through narrow slits to increase lift.

AVIAGRAPHICA

# BAe Canberra and Martin/GD B-57

## Canberra 1 to 24 (data for B(I).12 except where otherwise indicated)

**Origin:** English Electric Aviation (now British Aerospace), UK; built under licence by Government Aircraft Factories, Australia (B.20) and The Martin Company, USA (see separate entry).

**Type:** Two-seat interdictor.

**Engines:** Two 7,500lb (3402kg) thrust Rolls-Royce Avon 109 single-shaft turbojets, (PR.9) two 11,250lb (5100kg) Avon 206.

**Dimensions:** Span 63ft 11½in (19.5m); (PR.9) 67ft 10in; length 65ft 6in (19·95m); height 15ft 7in (4·72m).

**Weights:** Empty 23,173–27,950lb (10,400–12,700kg); loaded 43,000lb (19,504kg) maximum permissible 56,250lb (25,515kg).

**Performance:** Maximum speed 580mph (933km/h) at 30,000ft (9144m) or Mach 0·83; initial climb at maximum weight 3,400ft (1036m)/min; service ceiling 48,000ft (14,630m); range (typical mission at low level) 805 miles (1295km); ferry range 3,630 miles (5,842km).

**Armament:** Four 20mm Hispano cannon; three 1,000lb (454kg) bombs or sixteen 4·5in flares internally; two AS.30 missiles or two 1,000lb bombs or two packs of 37 rockets externally.

**History:** First flight (prototype) 13 May 1949; first service delivery October 1950; first flight of B(I) series 23 July 1954.

**Users:** Argentina, Ecuador, Ethiopia, France (trials), W Germany, India, New Zealand, Peru, S Africa, Sweden (trials), Venezuela, Zimbabwe-Rhodesia.

**Development:** When W. E. W. "Teddy" Petter joined English Electric at Preston as chief engineer he already had a scheme for a jet bomber. To meet specification B.3/45 he eventually planned a straightforward unswept aircraft with a broad wing for good behaviour at great heights, with two of the new axial jet engines centred on each wing giving a total of 15,000lb thrust. Like the Mosquito, the A.1 bomber was to be fast enough to escape interception, whilst carrying a 6,000lb bomb load over a radius of 750 nautical miles. It was to have a crew of two and a radar bomb sight for blind attacks in all conditions. The prototype amazed everyone with its low-level manoeuvrability, and the A.1, named Canberra, was a superb flying machine from the start. But the radar bombing system lagged years in development, and a new specification, B.5/47, had to be raised to cover a simpler visual bomber with a transparent nose and crew of three. This entered production without much more trouble and became the first axial-jet aircraft in the RAF. First Canberra B.2s were painted black on sides and under-surfaces, but this changed in 1952 to grey-blue, and the white serial number was

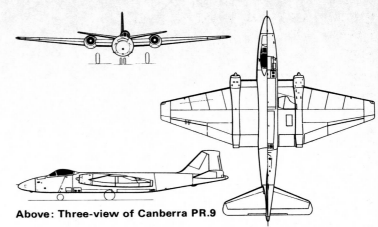

**Above: Three-view of Canberra PR.9**

painted extra-large to serve as a "buzz number" visible to fighter pilots from a safe distance. In February 1951 a B.2 set a transatlantic record flying out to Baltimore to serve as pattern aircraft for the Martin B-57 programme (see entry). The Korean war caused a sudden jump in orders, and Canberra B.2s were made by EECo and by Handley Page (75), Avro (75) and Short (60). The PR.3 was a reconnaissance version with longer fuselage for more fuel. The T.4 had side-by-side dual controls. The Mk 5 prototype introduced Avon 109 engines and integral wing tanks, and was to be a visual target marker. It led to the B.6, the heavier and more powerful replacement for the B.2. The corresponding reconnaissance version was the PR.7, from which was derived the much more powerful, long-span PR.9 developed and built by Short. Most versatile Canberra was the B(I).8, with offset pilot canopy and nav/bomb position in the nose. With four 20mm cannon (and ammunition for 55 seconds continuous firing) the Mk 8 also carried a wide range of under-wing missiles, bombs, tanks and special pods, and, like earlier versions, proved an export winner, particularly the B(I).12. Until they were ready the B(I).6 served in Germany in the multi-role tasks and also dashed to Kuwait in 1961. Later mark numbers include special trainers, electronic-warfare versions, target tugs, pilotless targets and, as one-off conversions, platforms for testing almost every British postwar engine, missile and airborne device. Total Canberra production was 925 in Britain; Australia made 49 B.20s for the RAAF.

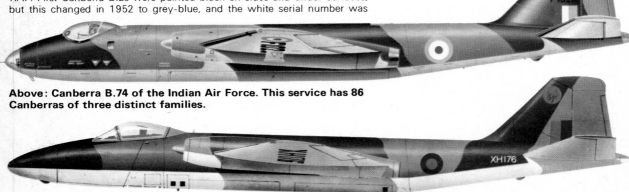

**Above: Canberra B.74 of the Indian Air Force. This service has 86 Canberras of three distinct families.**

**Photo below left: Canberra T.17 of No 360 Sqn, RAF Cottesmore. This, with the E.15, is a rebuild of earlier bomber versions, and 360 Sqn is joint-Services-operated.**

**Below: Canberra B.62 of 1 Escuadron de Bombardeo, Argentine Air Force. This again is a rebuild, but still a tactical bomber.**

**Above: The high-altitude Canberra PR.9 equips 39 Sqn at RAF Wyton. This version was built by Shorts.**

# B-57A to B-57G Night Intruder, RB-57A, D and F

**Origin:** Design, English Electric Aviation, UK; original US prime contractor, The Martin Co, Baltimore, USA; (RB-57F) GD/Fort Worth.

**Type:** Two-seat tactical attack and reconnaissance (RB versions, strategic reconnaissance at extreme altitude).

**Engines:** (A, B, C, E, G) two 7,220lb (3275kg) thrust Wright J65-5 (US Sapphire) single-shaft turbojets; (D) two 11,000lb (4990kg) Pratt & Whitney J57-37A two-shaft turbojets; (F) two 18,000lb (8165kg) Pratt & Whitney TF33-11A two-shaft turbofans and two 3,300lb (1500kg) Pratt & Whitney J60-9 single shaft turbojets.

**Dimensions:** Span (A, B, C, E, G) 64ft (19·5m); (D) 106ft (32·3m); (F) 122ft 5in (37·32m); length (A, B, C, D, E) 65ft 6in (19·96m); (G) 67ft (20·42m); (F) 69ft (21·03m); height (A, B, C, E, G) 15ft 7in (4·75m); (D) 14ft 10in (4·52m); (F) 19ft (5·79m).

**Weights:** Empty (A, B, C, E, typical) 26,800lb (12,200kg); (G) about 28,000lb (12,700kg); (D) 33,000lb (14,970kg); (F) about 36,000lb (16,330kg); maximum loaded (A) 51,000lb; (B, C, E, G) 55,000lb (24,950 kg); (D) not disclosed, (F) 63,000lb (28,576kg).

**Performance:** Maximum speed (A, B, C, E, G) 582mph (937km/h); (D, F) over 500mph (800km/h); initial climb (A, B, C, E, G) 3,500ft (1070m)/min; (D, F) about 4,000ft (1220m)/min; service ceiling (A, B, C, E, D) 48,000ft (14,630m); (D) 65,000ft (19,800m); (F) 75,000ft (22,860m); maximum range with combat load (high altitude) (A, B, C, E, G) 2,100 miles (3380kg); (D) about 3,000 miles (4828km); (F) about 3,700 miles (5955km).

**Armament:** (A and all RB versions) none; (B, C, E, G) provision for four 20mm or eight 0·5in guns fixed in outer wings (very rarely, other guns fixed in forward fuselage); internal bomb load of 5,000lb (2268kg) on rotary bomb door plus eight rockets, two 500lb bombs or other stores on under-wing pylons (while retaining tip tanks)

**History:** First flight (Canberra in UK) 13 May 1949; (production B-57A) 20 July 1953; (B) June 1954.

**Users:** Pakistan, Taiwan, USA (Air Force, ANG), Vietnam.

**Development:** In October 1949 Martin flew the extremely advanced XB-51 trijet attack bomber, but this proved to be inflexible and operationally unattractive. The much less advanced British Canberra, on the other hand, proved to have precisely the qualities the US Air Force was seeking, with near-perfect operational flexibility, versatility, outstanding manoeuvrability, long range and endurance and a good weapon load. The decision to adopt this foreign combat aircraft – a step unprecedented in the US since 1918 – was swiftly followed by choice of Martin and development of the B-57A as a version built to US standards with many small modifications. The main batch comprised B-57B tandem-seaters, with dual-C trainers and multi-role (tactical bomber/recce/trainer/tug) E models. Martin also made 20 grossly redesigned RB-57D reconnaissance aircraft with J57 engines on greatly extended wings. Though incapable of Canberra-style manoeuvres, nor of high speeds at low levels, the D flew many valuable multi-sensor missions over a great deal of Communist territory with the USAF and Nationalist Chinese. There were at least three D sub-types, some having counter-measures and sensing pods on the wing tips and/or tail and one version having large radomes at each end of the fuselage for strategic

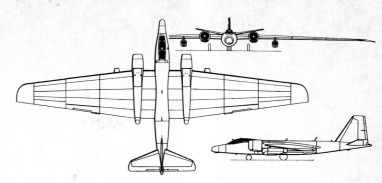

**Above: Three-view of General Dynamics RB-57F.**

electronic reconnaissance. Another B-57D task was to work with U-2Ds in upper-atmospheric sampling, but all of this type were grounded in 1963 as a result of structural fatigue. It was partly because of the interim nature of the D that, in 1960, General Dynamics was entrusted with the task of designing and building an even more dramatic high-altitude B-57 version, the F. Though the 21 of this type were not new aircraft, little of the old is evident. The wing is entirely new, with more than double the area of the original Canberra wing and a new fatigue-resistant multi-spar structure. Most of the fuselage is new, as is the vertical tail. There are four underwing hard points for pylons, two of which are often occupied by the J60 boost engine pods supplementing the large turbofans. The nose is packed with electronics, and multi-sensor equipment can be seen all over the fuselage. Various F models have operated from the United States, Europe and Middle East, Japan, Alaska, Panama, Argentina and possibly other countries. Meanwhile many of the B, C and E models have been updated by the fitment of modern night and all-weather sensing, target designation and weapon-aiming systems, the rebuilt aircraft being B-57G. Major new items are low-light TV, infra-red detector and laser ranging. About half the 403 B-57s served in the night attack role in Vietnam, the G being developed just too late for the conflict. Though 10 to 15 years old, the B-57 established an outstanding record in accurate weapon delivery under the most difficult conditions.

**Above: Reconditioned EB-57B of Kansas Air National Guard.**

**Above: B-57B of 31 Bomber Wing, Pakistan Air Force.**

**Below: B-57B of regular USAF unit drops eight 750lb bombs on a target in Vietnam in December 1967.**

# BAe Harrier and Sea Harrier

## Harrier GR.3 and T.4, AV-8A, TAV-8A and Sea Harrier FRS.1

**Origin:** Hawker Siddeley Aviation (now British Aerospace), UK.
**Type:** Single-seat tactical attack and reconnaissance; (T.4, TAV) dual trainer or special missions; (Sea Harrier) single-seat ship-based multi-role.
**Engine:** One 21,500lb (9752kg) thrust Rolls-Royce Pegasus 103 two-shaft vectored-thrust turbofan (US designation F402); (Sea H, Pegasus 104).
**Dimensions:** Span 25ft 3in (7·7m), (with bolt-on tips, 29ft 8in); length 45ft 6in (13·87m), (laser nose, 47ft 2in; two-seat trainers, 55ft 9½in; Sea Harrier, 48ft); height 11ft 3in (3·43m) (two-seat, 13ft 8in).
**Weights:** Empty (GR.1) 12,200lb (5533kg); (Sea H) 13,000lb (5897kg); (T) 13,600lb (6168kg); maximum (non-VTOL) 26,000lb (11,793kg).

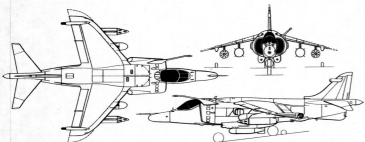

Above: Three-view drawing of Harrier GR.3 with FR probe, laser nose and (dotted) ferry tips.

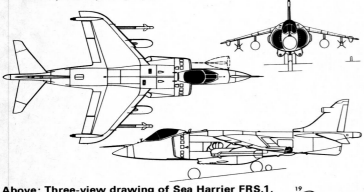

Above: Three-view drawing of Sea Harrier FRS.1.

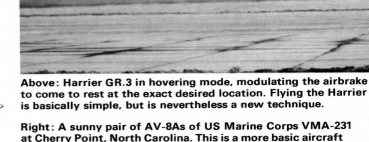

Above: Harrier GR.3 in hovering mode, modulating the airbrake to come to rest at the exact desired location. Flying the Harrier is basically simple, but is nevertheless a new technique.

Right: A sunny pair of AV-8As of US Marine Corps VMA-231 at Cherry Point, North Carolina. This is a more basic aircraft than the RAF GR.3, with no inertial system and armed with bombs and Sidewinders.

1 Starboard navigation light
2 Detachable wingtip
3 Outrigger wheel fairing
4 Hydraulic retraction jack
5 Leg fairing (upper section)
6 Starboard outrigger wheel
7 Leg fairing (lower section)
8 Telescopic oleo strut
9 Roll reaction valve
10 Roll reaction outlet
11 Aileron hinge fairing
12 Bonded aluminium honeycomb structure
13 Fuel jettison pipe
14 Aileron hinge
15 Tandem aileron jack and autostabilizer
16 Pylon spigot
17 Starboard outer pylon
18 Leading-edge duct to roll-reaction valve
19 Leading-edge wing fences
20 Riveted rolled stringers
21 Fuel/air valves

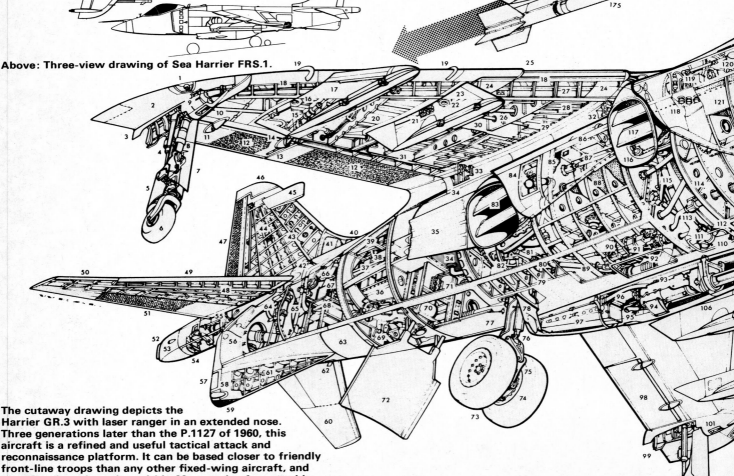

The cutaway drawing depicts the Harrier GR.3 with laser ranger in an extended nose. Three generations later than the P.1127 of 1960, this aircraft is a refined and useful tactical attack and reconnaissance platform. It can be based closer to friendly front-line troops than any other fixed-wing aircraft, and has often been in action within 90 seconds of a scramble call. In the British Sea Harrier and US Marine Corps AV-8B the basic concept is being taken further

22 Pylon spigot
23 Starboard inner pylon
24 Wing fuel tank
25 Wing leading-edge dog-tooth
26 Tank pressurizing air
27 Aileron control rod
28 Front spar web
29 Machined skin plank
30 Centre spar web

31 Rear spar web
32 Main wing attachment point
33 Rear spar/fuselage attachment point
34 Fuselage rear fuel tank
35 Rear nozzle heat shield
36 Vibration-isolating equipment rack
37 IFF-SSR transponder
38 TACAN trans-receiver

39 Ram-air turbine
40 HF tuner
41 HF notch aerial
42 Tailfin attachment bracket
43 Tailfin structure
44 Total temperature sensor
45 ECM pod
46 VHF aerial
47 Rudder
48 Tailplane front spar

61 Ventral fin structure
62 UHF stand-by aerial
63 Rear fuselage access hatch
64 Hydraulic filter No 2 (tailplane)
65 Tandem tailplane jack
66 Rudder cable tensioner
67 UHF stand-by
68 Batteries shelf
69 Airbrake jack

86 Reservoir No 2 system
87 Rear nozzle bearings
88 Starboard centre fuel tank

115 Intermediate chain
116 Chain and sprocket nozzle actuation
117 Fan air nozzle
118 Ground servicing points No 2 system: hydraulics, fuel and air supply external connections
119 GTS/APU
120 Venting air
121 Titanium heat shield (internal)
122 Rolls-Royce Bristol Pegasus 103 engine (buried)
123 Starboard front fuel tank
124 Machined nose-gear/keel beams
125 Nose-gear fairing
126 Nosewheel steering motor
127 Shock absorber strut
128 Nosewheel
129 Nosewheel fork
130 Landing lamp
131 Port front fuel tank
132 Supplementary air doors (free-floating)
133 Port intake
134 Pre-closing nose-gear door
135 Bleed-air duct
136 Nosewheel steering hydraulics accumulator
137 Nosewheel input mechanism
138 Control cables
139 Intake centre-body
140 First-stage fan
141 Supplementary air doors (free-floating)
142 Boundary air bleed doors (suction-operated)
143 Cabin air-conditioning and pressurization plant
144 Entry hand/footholds
145 Seat mounting frame
146 Nozzle actuation cable tension regulator
147 TACAN aerial
148 Bulkhead labyrinth seal
149 Pitch reaction valve ducting
150 Rudder quadrant
151 Starboard instrument console (TACAN and IFF control panels)
152 Top longeron
153 Canopy MDC (miniature detonating cord)
154 Martin-Baker Type 9A rocket-assisted ejection seat
155 Canopy
156 Machined windscreen frame and arch
157 Birdstrike-proof windscreen
158 Rear-view mirror
159 Head-up display
160 Instrument panel
161 Rudder pedals
162 Front pressure bulkhead
163 Pitch reaction valve
164 Nose cone attachment spigots
165 IFF aerial
166 Port-facing camera
167 Circular camera port
168 Nose cone
169 Ferranti Laser Ranger and Marked Target Seeker array
170 Laser mirror
171 Pitot boom
172 Outer weapons pylons
173 Adaptor shoe
174 Missile launch-rail
175 Sidewinder air-to-air missiles (USMC only)

49 Tailplane nose ribs
50 Tailplane extension ribs
51 Bonded aluminium honeycomb structure
52 Tail antenna
53 Tail navigation light
54 Pitch and yaw-reaction valve
55 Rudder/yaw-reaction nozzle linkage
56 Pitch and yaw-reaction valve ducting
57 IFF notch aerial
58 Compass flux valve
59 Plastic tail bumper
60 Port all-moving tailplane

70 Lox container (1.1 Imp gal/ 5 l)
71 Extruded L-section longeron
72 Airbrake (extended)
73 Rigid live-axle mounted mainwheels
74 Multi-disc brakes
75 Torque links
76 Mainwheel leg
77 Pre-closing mainwheel door
78 Mainwheel leg fairing
79 Machined main gear beams
80 Rear bevel gearbox
81 Transverse drive shafts
82 Compensating engine rear support member
83 Rear exhaust nozzle
84 No 2 hydraulic reservoir nitrogen charging connection
85 Titanium heat shield (internal)

89 Longitudinal drive shaft to rear nozzles
90 Gearbox
91 Master shut-off (butterfly) valve (reaction control system)
92 Nozzle rotation air motors
93 Port 30-mm Aden cannon
94 Case ejection
95 Link ejection
96 Rigid feed chute
97 Ammunition box
98 Port aileron
99 Outrigger wheel fairing
100 Port outrigger wheel
101 Roll reaction outlet
102 Port navigation light
103 Port outer pylon
104 Port inner pylon
105 Ejector release unit
106 Port cannon fairing (starboard weapon deleted for clarity)
107 Blast suppressor
108 Frangible cap fairing
109 Front attachment point
110 Roll reaction valve ducting
111 Air filter
112 Front bevel gearbox
113 Transverse drive shafts
114 Fabricated engine front mounting frame

**Hawker Siddeley AV-8A of US Marine Corps VMA-513, Beaufort, South Carolina.**

21

**Performance:** Maximum speed 737mph (1186km/h, Mach 0·972) at low level; maximum dive Mach number, 1·3; initial climb (VTOL weight) 50,000ft (15,240m)/min; service ceiling, over 50,000ft (15,240m); tactical radius on strike mission without drop tanks (hi-lo-hi) 260 miles (418km); ferry range 2,070 miles (3330km).

**Armament:** All external, with many options. Under-fuselage strakes both replaceable by pod containing one 30mm Aden or similar gun, with 150 rounds. Five or seven stores pylons, centre and two inboard each rated at 2,000lb (907kg), outers at 650lb (295kg) and tips (if used) at 220lb (100kg) for Sidewinder or similar. Normal load 5,300lb (2400kg), but 8,000lb (3630kg) has been flown.

**History:** First hover (P.1127) 21 October 1960; first flight (P.1127) 13 March 1961; first flight (Kestrel) 13 February 1964; (development Harrier) 31 August 1966; (Harrier GR.1) 28 December 1967; (T.2) 24 April 1969; (Sea Harrier FRS.1) 20 August 1978; squadron service (GR.1) 1 April 1969; squadron service (GR.1) 1 April 1969.

**Users:** Spain (Navy, AV-8A), UK (RAF, Royal Navy), USA (Marine Corps).

**Development:** In the 1950s the realisation that the thrust/weight ratio of the gas turbine made possible a new class of high-speed jets having VTOL (vertical takeoff and landing) capability led to a rash of unconventional prototypes and research machines. Only one has led to a useful combat aircraft. It was the P.1127, designed by Camm's team in 1957-59 around a unique engine, planned at Bristol by Stanley Hooker, in which the fan and core flows are discharged through four nozzles which, by means of chain drives from a single pneumatic motor, can be swivelled to point downwards, to lift the aircraft, or point to the rear, for propulsion. Gradually the P.1127 was transformed into the Kestrel, which equipped a UK/USA/German evaluation squadron in 1965. This was further developed into the Harrier (the much bigger, Mach 2, P.1154 for the RAF and RN having been cancelled in 1965). Powered by a Pegasus 101 rated at 19,000lb, the GR.1 was capable of flying useful combinations of fuel and stores out of any hastily prepared site and did more than any other aircraft to explore the advantages and problems of operational deployment of combat aircraft well away from any airfield. Numerous flights were made from a wide variety of naval vessels and record flights were made from the centre of London to the centre of New York and vice versa. The GR.1A had the 20,000lb Mk 102 engine and at this thrust the Harrier was adopted as the AV-8A by the US Marine Corps in both beach assault and defensive roles. All RAF and USMC aircraft have been re-engined with the Pegasus 103, giving a payload/range performance adequate for a wide spectrum of missions, many of which cannot be flown by any other aircraft. Using VIFF (vectoring in forward flight) the Harrier can fly "impossible" manoeuvres and has proved itself an extremely tricky customer in a dogfight. This is not its main mission, however, and the RAF Harrier GR.3 (92 built) is primarily a tactical attack platform with Ferranti INAS (inertial nav/attack system) and laser ranger. The USMC AV-8A (112, plus six for Spain named Matador) does not have either of these equipments but carries Sidewinder air/air missiles. Including two-seaters, production by 1977 amounted to 231. In Britain the main effort is completing development of the redesigned Sea Harrier, which should fly in 1977. The Royal Navy will deploy 24 from throughdeck cruisers and possibly other ships, and several other navies are discussing possible orders. The Sea Harrier has a completely new nose, with raised cockpit, Blue Fox radar, much enhanced systems and equipment and weapons for surface attack, reconnaissance, anti-submarine warfare and air combat. Since 1975 talks have been held with China, which is interested in buying a large number of Harriers.

**Above: Harrier GR.3 carrying four Matra 155 launchers lets go the 19 SNEB 68mm rockets from No 3. Such missiles are of value chiefly in the air/surface role.**

**Top: The third Full Scale Development example of the McDonnell Douglas/BAe AV-8B photographed in February 1982. Although derived from the Harrier I/AV-8A, the latest version is a totally new aircraft incorporating improvements in almost every aspect of the design, including the vastly superior view from the cockpit.**

**Centre: The same aircraft shows one of the advantages of the big new wing, built of graphite composites and with an essentially limitless fatigue life: as well as housing more fuel, it provides six stores stations — eight in the RAF GR.5 — which can accommodate a wide variety of armaments, including up to 16 500lb (227kg) bombs.**

**Above: In this view of the third FSD AV-8B note the wing leading-edge root extension (Lerx) and the long-scarf front nozzles of the Pegasus engine. The latter have a more dramatic effect on aircraft performance than their simple shape might suggest.**

# BAe Hawk

## P.1182 Hawk T.1

**Origin:** British Aerospace, UK.
**Type:** Two-seat trainer and tactical multi-role.
**Engine:** One 5,340lb (2422kg) Rolls-Royce/Turboméca Adour 151 two-shaft turbofan.
**Dimensions:** Span 30ft 10in (9·4m); length (over probe) 39ft 2½in (11·95m); height 13ft 5in (4·09m).
**Weights:** Empty 7,450lb (3379kg); loaded (trainer, clean) 12,000lb (5443kg), (attack mission) 16,260lb (7375kg).
**Performance:** Maximum speed 630mph (1014km/h) at low level; Mach number in shallow dive, 1·1; initial climb 6,000ft (1830m)/min; service ceiling 50,000ft (15,240m); range on internal fuel 750 miles (1207km); endurance with external fuel 3 hr.
**Armament:** Three or five hard-points (two outboard being optional) each rated at 1,000lb (454kg); centreline point normally equipped with 30mm gun pod and ammunition.
**History:** First flight 21 August 1974; service delivery 1976.
**Users:** Finland, Indonesia, Kenya, UK (RAF).

**Development:** The only new all-British military aircraft for 15 years, the Hawk serves as a model of the speed and success that can be achieved when an experienced team is allowed to get on with the job. To some degree it owes its existence to the escalation of the Jaguar to a power and weight category well above that economic for use as a pure trainer. Britain never participated in the Franco-German Alpha Jet programme and instead played off the two British airframe builders, finally making a choice between the Adour without afterburner and the less powerful Viper 632. With the Adour, the Hawk had a chance to be a world-beater, and backed by an immediate RAF order for 175 the Hawker Siddeley plants rapidly completed design, tooled for fast manufacture with assembly at Dunsfold and completed development of the RAF T.1 version all within the first two years of the programme. By October 1976 a dozen aircraft had flown and deliveries had begun to the RAF to replace the Gnat, Hunter and, eventually, Jet Provost, in roles ranging from basic flying to advanced weapon training. Thanks to very rapid development the Hawk was kept to the original budget and price and by late 1979 nearly all the 175 aircraft for the RAF had been delivered. So pleased is the RAF that a repeat-order has been requested, though funds are awaited. A proportion of Hawks may be single-seat dedicated close-support machines.

**Above: Most of the 175 Hawks for RAF Training Command are finished in this colour scheme, for pilot training.**

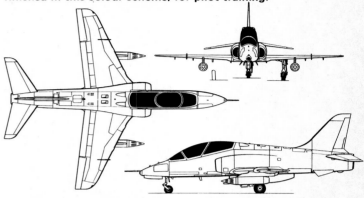

**Above: Three-view of Hawk with centreline gun and rockets.**

**Below: Several air forces are negotiating for multi-role tactical Hawks with two extra outboard pylons and total external weapon load of 5,600lb (2540kg).**

# BAe Lightning

## Lightning F.1 to 6 and export versions (data for F.6)

**Origin:** English Electric Aviation (now British Aerospace), UK.
**Type:** Single-seat all-weather interceptor.
**Engines:** Two 15,680lb (7112kg) thrust Rolls-Royce Avon 302 augmented turbojets.
**Dimensions:** span 34ft 10in (10·6m); length 53ft 3in (16·25m); height 19ft 7in (5·95m).
**Weights:** Empty about 28,000lb (12,700kg); loaded 50,000lb (22,680kg).
**Performance:** Maximum speed 1,500mph (2415km/h) at 40,000ft (12,200m); initial climb 50,000ft (15,240m)/min; service ceiling over 60,000ft (18,290m); range without overwing tanks 800 miles (1290km).
**Armament:** Interchangeable packs for two all-attitude Red Top or stern-chase Firestreak guided missiles; option of two 30mm Aden cannon in forward part of belly tank; export versions up to 6,000lb (2722kg) bombs or other offensive stores above and below wings.
**History:** First flight (P.1B) 4 April 1957; (first production F.1) 30 October 1959; (first F.6) 17 April 1964.
**Users:** Kuwait, Saudi Arabia, UK.

**Development:** As he had been with the Canberra, "Teddy" Petter was again moving spirit behind the award, in 1947, of a study contract for a supersonic research aircraft. Later this was built and flown as the P.1 of August 1954, exceeding Mach 1 on two crude unaugmented Sapphire engines mounted one above and behind the other and fed by a plain nose inlet. In mid-1949 specification F.23/49 was issued for a supersonic fighter, and after complete redesign the P.1B was produced and flown in 1957. This had a new fuselage with a two-shock intake, the central cone being intended to house Ferranti Airpass radar. The Avon engines were fitted with primitive afterburning, allowing a speed of Mach 2 to be attained on 25 November 1958. Helped by 20 pre-production aircraft, the Lightning F.1 was cleared for service in 1960. Though relatively complicated, so that the flying rate and maintenance burden were terrible in comparison with more modern aircraft, these supersonic all-weather interceptors at last gave the RAF a modern fighter with radar, guided missiles (heat-homing Firestreaks) and supersonic performance. Production was held back by the belief that all manned fighters were obsolete (as clearly set forth in the Defence White Paper of April 1957), but the Treasury were persuaded to allow the improved F.2 to be built in 1961 with fully variable afterburner and all-weather navigation. Eventually, as the error of the 1957 doctrine became apparent, the Mk 3 was allowed in 1964, with more powerful engines, more fuel, bigger fin, collision-course fire-control and allattitude Red Top missiles; but it was decided to fit no guns, earlier marks having had two 30mm Aden cannon. Finally, in 1965, the belated decision was taken to follow the advice of BAC and almost double the fuel capacity and also fit the kinked and cambered wing (first flown in 1956) to improve operation at much increased weights. The T.4 and T.5 are dual conversion trainers equivalent to the F.2 and F.3. For Saudi Arabia and Kuwait, BAC paid for development of the Lightning as a multi-role fighter and attack aircraft, adding 57 to the production total to bring it up to 338.

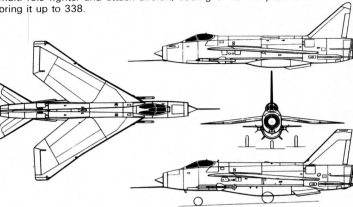

**Above: Lightning F.6, with upper side elevation showing F.1.**

**Left: Lightning F.6 as originally in service with No 5 Sqn, RAF, showing unpainted finish and Firestreak missiles. The flight-refuelling probe can be seen attached beneath the left wing. It does not impair the Lightning's dogfighting capability.**

**Right and below: The Lightning F.2A is a rebuild of the early Mk 2 almost up to F.6 standard. Both the 92 Sqn aircraft (right) and the 19 Sqn example (below, at Warton) introduced painted upper surfaces rendering them less easy to see from above.**

# BAe Nimrod

## Nimrod MR.1, MR.2, R.1 and AEW.3

**Origin:** Hawker Siddeley Aviation (British Aerospace), UK.
**Type:** (MR) maritime reconnaissance and anti-submarine aircraft, with operating crew of 12, with several secondary roles; (R) electronic reconnaissance and countermeasures.
**Engines:** Four 11,995lb (5441kg) thrust Rolls-Royce Spey 250 two-shaft turbofans.
**Dimensions:** Span 114ft 10in (35m); length 126ft 9in (38·63m); (R.1) 118ft; height 29ft 8½in (9·08m).
**Weights:** Empty (MR, typical) 92,000lb (41,730kg); loaded 192,000lb (87,090kg).
**Performance:** Maximum speed 575mph (926km/h), economical transit speed 490mph (787km/h); climb and ceiling, not disclosed; mission endurance 12 hours; ferry range, typically 5,755 miles (9265km).
**Armament:** 50ft (15m) weapon bay capable of carrying very wide range of stores, including AS torpedoes, mines, depth bombs, nuclear weapons, conventional bombs and fuel tanks; two (optionally four) underwing pylons for air-to-surface missiles such as Martel or AS.12.
**History:** First flight (aerodynamic prototype) 23 May 1967; (production MR.1) 28 June 1968; service delivery 2 October 1969.
**User:** UK (RAF).

**Development:** Though it is derived from the Comet civil transport the Nimrod has proved an outstandingly successful aircraft. The original MR.1 was tailored to an equipment standard which, for budgetary reasons, fell short of the ideal, but still combined very complete ASW (anti-submarine warfare) sensing systems with digital and analog computers, advanced

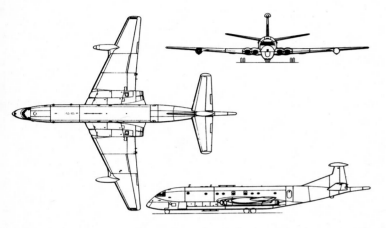

Above: Three-view of Nimrod MR.1 or 2 (R.1 has short tailcone).

Above: Few aircraft have been worked harder than the Nimrod MR.1 squadrons of the RAF. This aircraft taking off from Gibraltar is from 206 Sqn, RAF Kinloss, Morayshire (Scotland). It was participating in NATO Exercise Open Gate.

Below: On any number of engines from one upwards, the Nimrod is a splendid aircraft. No other ocean patroller offers such effortless performance, and in 1977-79 the RAF MR.1 force is being updated internally to improve combat effectiveness still further.

►tactical displays and comprehensive inertial, doppler and three other navigation systems. The best thing about the MR.1 is the aircraft itself, which surpasses all other aircraft in use for ocean patrol in speed, quietness, flight performance, reliability and all-round mission efficiency. In emergency it can be fitted with 45 passenger seats in the rear compartment without significantly disturbing operational equipment. The RAF force of 46, which have operated around the clock in often extremely severe conditions, are being completely modernised at their half-life point in 1977-78, with new Searchwater radar, greatly increased computer capacity and a new acoustic processing system matched with the Barra sonobuoy. The R.1 force of three aircraft are specially equipped for sensing, recording and emitting electromagnetic and other data. Since 1973 a detailed study has been made of a Nimrod AEW (airborne early warning) aircraft as a replacement for the Shackleton. Distinguished by large radomes at nose and tail, this machine has outstanding capabilities, especially in the European and overwater environment. Preliminary trials with the nose aerial were flown with a Comet and rebuilding of the first Nimrod to AEW.3 standard began in September 1978. Programme cost is estimated at £400 million.

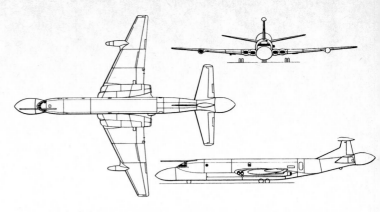

Three-view of Nimrod AEW.3. All 11 of this type are being rebuilt from existing MR.1 airframes. It is planned that the AEW force should start replacing the Shackleton AEW.2 in late 1981.

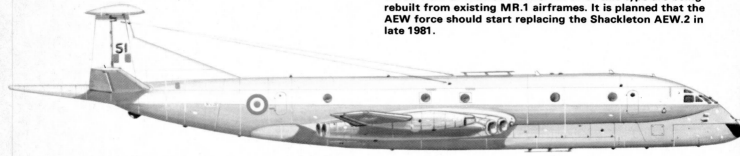

**Above: Nimrod MR.1 of 236 OCU (fin number is last two digits of serial).**

**Left: Pilots and (left) flight engineer in a 201 Sqn Nimrod operating out of Kinloss. Bonedomes are not worn, and in endurance flying on two engines the flight deck is virtually devoid of background noise.**

1 Dielectric radome
2 Taxi lamp
3 ASV-21D search and weather radar (MR.2, Searchwater)
4 Radome hoist point
5 Front pressure bulkhead
6 Windscreen for all-weather use
7 Four wipers
8 Instrument panel coaming
9 Co-pilot's seat
10 Eyebrow window
11 Pilot's seat
12 Pitot head
13 Twin nosewheels
14 Sonics homing aerial
15 Doppler bay
16 Forward radio pack
17 Autolycus diesel sniffer
18 Autolycus equipment rack
19 Port D.C. electrics crate
20 Engineer's station
21 Emergency escape hatch
22 Starboard D.C. electrics crate
23 Crew entry door
24 Periscopic sextant
25 Equipment systems crate
26 Toilet
27 Ground supply socket
28 Weapons-pannier door ground control

45 Radio operator
46 Tactical commander
47 Sonics station (2)
48 Sonics operators (2)
49 ASV operator
50 Partition
51 Space provision for extra sensor operator's station
52 Radio trough
53 Sonics cupboard
54 Port AC electrics crate
55 Starboard AC electrics crate
56 Aft radio rack
57 ESM/MAD operator
58 Machined inner-wing skin
59 Undercarriage bay upper panel

77 Flap inner section
78 Inboard airbrake (upper surface only)
79 Blackout curtain
80 Emergency escape panels
81 Fuselage frames
82 Electrics trough
83 Dinette
84 Fixed galley
85 Partition with folding door

29 Weapons-pannier door
30 Door strut
31 Mixed ASW weapons load
32 Tank blow-off
33 'On-top' sight
34 Port beam lookout's seat
35 Domed observation window (hinged, pressure-bearing, with sight linked to computer)
36 Starboard beam lookout's seat
37 Domed observation window (fixed)
38 Analog computer rack
39 Digital computer rack
40 Blackout curtain
41 Map projector station
42 Routine navigator
43 Plot display
44 Tactical navigator

60 Starboard weapons pylon
61 Flow spoiler
62 Searchlight, 70 million candle power
63 External fuel tank
64 Wing bumper
65 Fixed slot
66 Integral fuel tanks
67 Skin butt-joint rib
68 Over-wing filler
69 Starboard navigation light
70 Wingtip fuel vent
71 Starboard aileron
72 Aileron tab
74 Flap outer section
74 Airbrake (upper and lower surfaces)
75 Fuel dump pipes
76 Fuel vent

86 Size A sonobuoy stowage
87 Underfloor bag-type keel tanks
88 Port lookout and stores-loader
89 Starboard lookout and stores-loader
90 Observation ports (port and starboard)
91 Pressurized launchers
92 Rotary launchers
93 Ready-use oxygen stowage
94 Intercom panel
95 Stores control panel
96 Emergency doo
97 Hand extinguisher
98 Underfloor parachute stowage
99 First-aid kit
100 Escape rope stowage
101 Camera magazine stowage

102 Retro-launcher (cancels airspeed)
103 F.135 camera hatch
104 Hat-rack
105 ESM amplifier
106 Equipment cooling fans
107 Rear pressure bulkhead
108 Dorsal fin
109 HF aerial
110 Starboard tailplane
111 VOR aerial
112 Dielectric fairing
113 ESM aerial
114 Dummy ESM (test) aerial
115 Rudder
116 Fin structure
117 Dielectric tailcone
118 MAD aerial
119 Elevator tab
120 Port elevator
121 VOR aerial

122 Tailplane structure
123 Tail bumper/fuselage vent
124 Fin/fuselage frame
125 De-icing conduit
126 Rudder and elevator linkage
127 APU
128 APU and aft fuselage access hatch
129 Safe
130 Liquid oxygen pack
131 F.126 camera access hatch
132 Intercom panel
133 Main door
134 Ground-operated doors (rear loading of stores)
135 Tailpipes
136 Dinghy stowage
137 Thrust reverser (outboard only)
138 Rear spar/fuselage attachment point

139 Rolls-Royce Spey 250 turbofan (12,140 lb/5,506 kg thrust)
140 Inboard engine bay (engine not shown)
141 Heat exchanger
142 Front spar/fuselage attachment point
143 Landing/taxi light
144 Anti-iced intakes
145 Ram air to heat exchanger
146 Flow spoiler
147 Undercarriage well
148 Weapon pylon (two Aérospatiale AS.12 missiles)
149 External fuel tank
150 Access panels
151 Wing structure
152 Port navigation light
153 Wingtip vent
154 Port aileron

Above: Typical of the daily routine missions of the RAF Nimrod MR force is the finding and shadowing of Soviet surface warships and submarines. This MR.1 is trailing the helicopter cruiser *Leningrad,* a task which calls for the maximum ESM capability as well as considerable computer memory and processing capacity. With withdrawal from Malta the RAF has four squadrons (42, 120, 201 and 206), based at St Mawgan and Kinloss.

Above: Nerve centre of a Nimrod. The routine navigator (left) gets the aircraft to where the action is—which it can do faster than other ASW aircraft —whereupon the tactical navigator goes to war and builds marvellous pictures on his 24-inch display.

155  Aileron tab
156  Flap outer section
157  Airbrake (upper and lower surfaces)
158  Dump pipes
159  Vent
160  Flap structure

Above: The cutaway drawing shows all salient features of the standard MR.1 or 2 Nimrod, which in practice seldom carry external weapons such as the small wire-guided AS.12. All MR.1 Nimrods are being recycled back through the Woodford factory to emerge in updated MR.2 form, with EMI Searchwater radar with Ferranti FM 1600D computer, a 920C central processor with 256K words, and the new Marconi-Elliott AQS-901 acoustic system (compatible with Barra sonobuoys) with two more 920C computers.

# BAe Strikemaster and 145

## BAC 145 and Strikemaster

**Origin:** Hunting/BAC (now British Aerospace), UK.
**Type:** Two-seat light tactical aircraft and trainer.
**Engine:** 3,410lb (1547kg) thrust Rolls-Royce Viper 535 turbojet.
**Dimensions:** Span 36ft 10in (11·23m); length 33ft 8½in (10·27m); height 10ft 11½in (3·34m).
**Weights:** Empty 6,270lb (2840kg); loaded (clean) 9,200lb (4170kg); maximum 11,500lb (5210kg).
**Performance:** Maximum speed 481mph (774km/h); maximum speed at sea level 450mph (726km/h); initial climb (max fuel, clean) 5,250ft (1600m)/min; service ceiling 44,000ft (13,410m); ferry range 1,615 miles (2600km); combat radius with 3,300lb weapon load 145 miles (233km).
**Armament:** Two 7·62mm FN machine guns fixed firing forwards with 550 rounds each; wide range of stores to maximum of 3,000lb (1360kg) on four underwing strongpoints.
**History:** First flight (Jet Provost) 16 June 1954; (Strikemaster) 26 October 1967; first delivery 1968.
**Users:** (Jet Provost) Iraq, Kuwait, Rhodesia, S Yemen, Sri Lanka, Sudan, UK, Venezuela; (Strikemaster) Ecuador, Kenya, Kuwait, New Zealand, Oman, Saudi Arabia, Singapore, Sudan, S Yemen.

**Development:** The Percival Provost basic trainer flew in February 1950. Hunting then produced a jet version, and flew this in June 1954. Subsequently the Hunting (later BAC) Jet Provost became a successful basic trainer made in great numbers for the RAF and many overseas countries, and more powerful pressurised versions are still one of BAC's current products. From this was developed the BAC.145 multi-role trainer/attack aircraft, which in turn was developed into the highly refined Strikemaster. With a more powerful Viper engine, the Strikemaster proved to be a great world-

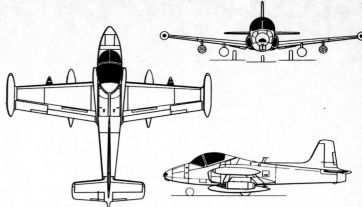

**Above: Three-view of basic BAC 167 Strikemaster with rocket pods and tanks.**

wide success. It has side-by-side ejection seats, and the ability to operate from the roughest airstrip whilst carrying a combat load three times a typical bomber's load in the 1930s and any desired equipment fit. The Strikemaster has set a world record for the number of repeat orders placed by its export customers. In early 1977 there were no plans to install the most powerful Viper, the Mk 632, because this would reduce time between overhauls and increase cost without meeting any requirement expressed by a customer. In 1973-76 BAC refurbished 177 RAF Jet Provosts, in the course of which VOR, DME and ILS were installed.

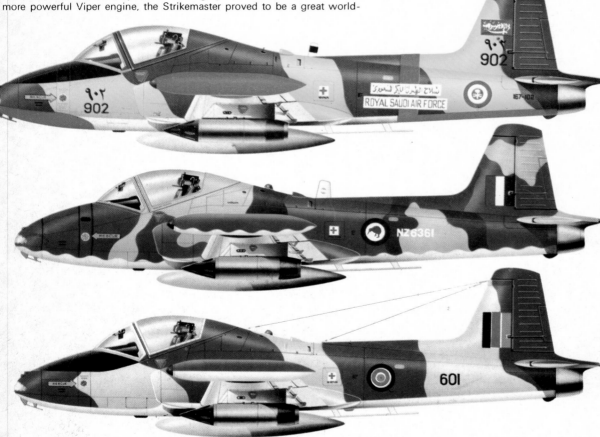

**Left: Strikemaster Mk 80 of the Royal Saudi Air Force, with typical pylon loads of tanks and 18-round Matra rocket launchers. BAC delivered 25 to this customer in 1968–69, followed by ten Mk 80A. Strikemasters have proved extremely popular among Middle East air forces.**

**Left: Strikemaster Mk 88 of Royal New Zealand Air Force. The initial batch of ten led to a repeat order for another six used for advanced weapon training.**

**Left: Strikemaster Mk 87 of Kenya Air Force. Six were delivered and five are currently in use as attack/trainer aircraft. The KAF is soon to have to learn the more costly and complex F-5E.**

**Left: Strikemaster Mk 82 of the Sultan of Oman's Air Force, taxiing out with 1,000lb bombs and 80mm Sura rockets. The SOAF received 12, followed by eight Mk 82A, and though several have been shot down (some by SA-7 missiles) these tough and simple machines have proved ideal in helping to defeat the Dhofar rebellion, which was officially declared ended in 1976.**

# BAe Victor

## H.P.80 Victor 1, 1A and 2

**Origin:** Handley Page Ltd, UK; K.2, rebuilt by Hawker Siddeley (now British Aerospace).

**Type:** (B.1, 1A and 2) five-seat strategic bomber; (K.1A and 2) four-seat air-refuelling tanker; (SR.2) strategic reconnaissance.

**Engines:** (1, 1A) four 11,000lb (4990kg) thrust Rolls-Royce (previously Armstrong Siddeley and then Bristol Siddeley) Sapphire 202 single-shaft turbojets; (2) four 17,500lb (7938kg) thrust Rolls-Royce Conway 103 two-shaft turbofans; (B.2R, SR.2, K.2) 20,600lb (9344kg) thrust Conway 201.

**Dimensions:** Span (1) 110ft (33·53m); (2) 120ft (36·58m); length 114ft 11in (35·05m); height (1) 28ft 1½in (8·59m); (2) 30ft 1½in (9·2m).

**Weights:** Empty (1) 79,000lb (35,834kg); (2) 91,000lb (41,277kg); loaded (1) 180,000lb (81,650kg); (2) 233,000lb (101,150kg).

**Performance:** Maximum speed (both) about 640 mph (1030km/h, Mach 0·92) above 36,000ft; service ceiling (1) 55,000ft (16,764m); (2) 60,000ft (18,290m); range (1) 2,700 miles (4345km); (2) 4,600 miles (7400km).

**Armament:** No defensive armament except ECM; internal weapon bay for various nuclear or conventional weapons, including 35 1,000lb (454kg) bombs; (B.2 and 2R) provision for launching one Blue Steel Mk 1 air-to-surface missile carried semi-externally beneath fuselage; (K.2) none.

**History:** First flight (1) 24 December 1952; (production B.1) 1 February 1956; (2) 20 February 1959; (K.1A conversion) 28 April 1965; (K.2 conversion) 1 March 1972; final delivery of new aircraft 2 May 1963.

**User:** UK.

**Development:** Designed to Specification B.35/46, the same as the Vulcan, the Handley Page H.P.80 was expected to fly so fast and high as to be virtually immune to interception. To achieve the highest cruising Mach number the wing was designed to what was called a "crescent" shape, with a sharply swept but thick inner section housing the buried engines and progressively less swept but thinner outer panels, the structure being largely of light-alloy double-skin sandwich with corrugated or honeycomb filling. As a technical achievement the aircraft was superb. Named Victor it was the third and last of the V-bombers to go into service with RAF Bomber Command in 1955-58, but it took so long to develop that, by that time it

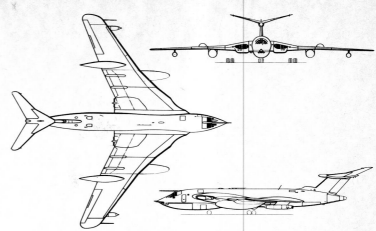

**Above: Three-view of Handley Page (Hawker Siddeley) Victor K.2.**

entered service, it could be intercepted by fighters or shot down by missiles and the number ordered was so small the cost was high. To offer better protection the B.1 was brought up to B.1A standard with much enhanced ECM and survivors of the 50 built were in 1965-67 converted as K.1A tankers. The much more powerful B.2, with completely redesigned airframe and systems, offered a great increase in all-round performance, but at height was no less vulnerable in penetrating hostile airspace and by 1964 was consigned to the low-level role, carrying the big Blue Steel missile. Several of the 30 built were converted as SR.2 strategic reconnaissance photographic aircraft and in 1973-75 the final 20 were converted as three-point K.2 tankers. This work was done by Hawker Siddeley at Woodford, the old Handley Page firm having gone into liquidation in 1970. Delivery of the K.2 began in May 1974, and by 1977 the last K.1 was withdrawn.

**Above: Victor K.2 of 55 Sqn, RAF Strike Command.**

**Above: Victor B.2 (with Blue Steel missile) as formerly in service with 139 Sqn, RAF.**

**Below: One of the early Victor K.1A tankers, in service with 57 Sqn, pipes fuel to a thirsty Buccaneer. Though fitted with three hose-reels (some have only two) the K.1A has gradually been phased out as the much superior K.2 Victor comes into service.**

# CASA C-101 Aviojet

## C-101

**Origin:** Construcciones Aeronauticas SA, Getafe, Spain.
**Type:** Basic and advanced trainer, attack and reconnaissance aircraft.
**Engine:** One Garrett-AiResearch TFE 731-3 two-shaft turbofan rated at 3,700lb (1678kg).
**Dimensions:** Span 34ft 9½in (10·60m); length 40ft 2¼in (12·25m); height 14ft 1¼in (4·30m).
**Weights:** Empty (fully equipped) 6,570lb (2980kg); maximum loaded 10,360lb (4700kg).
**Performance:** (Estimated at 4700kg) maximum speed at 25,000ft (7620m) 494mph (795km/h); limiting Mach number 0·80; initial climb 3,660ft (1116m)/min; service ceiling 43,000ft (13,100m); take-off over 50ft (15m) 2,950ft (900m) (landing distance 2,165ft, 660m); maximum range (presumably with external fuel) 1,883 miles (3030km).
**Armament:** Seven hardpoints for total external load of 4,740lb (2150kg), including multisensor reconnaissance pods, gunpacks or ECM payloads.
**History:** Development contract September 1975; first flight 27 June 1977; service delivery 1980.
**User:** Spain.

**Development:** The EdA (Ejercito del Aire, Spanish AF) is funding at a cost of 1,297 million pesetas the development of this completely new multi-role trainer and tactical aircraft to replace the E-14 and C-10 versions of the Saeta. Unlike other aircraft in this category the C-101 uses an off-the-shelf civil turbofan of high by-pass ratio, which will reduce noise and smoke, and give good fuel economy at all heights, at the cost of reduced speeds and poor high-altitude performance. Northrop and MBB are participating in the programme, mainly through provision of design and development skills and facilities. Six prototypes are being built, two for static/fatigue testing, plus 60 for EdA schools.

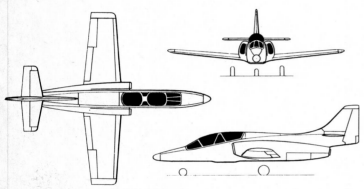

**Three-view of CASA C-101 (provisional).**

Above and top: Contrasting colour schemes on two early examples of the CASA C-101 Aviojet, designated E-25 in Spanish Air Force service. A total of 88 were acquired by the Ejercito del Aire, equipping the Academia del Aire and the 41ºGrupo, while an armed export version, designated C-101CC, has been ordered by Chile.

# CASA C.212 Aviocar

## C.212 (T.12)

**Origin:** CASA, Madrid, Spain; licence-built by Lipnur, Indonesia.
**Type:** Utility transport.
**Engines:** Two 776ehp Garrett-AiResearch TPE331-251C single-shaft turboprops.
**Dimensions:** Span 62ft 4in (19·0m); length 49ft 10½in (15·2m); height 20ft 8in (6·3m).
**Weights:** Empty 8,157lb (3700kg); maximum useful load 4,410lb (2000kg); maximum loaded 13,889lb (6300kg).
**Performance:** Maximum speed 230mph (370km/h) at 12,000ft; economical cruising speed at 12,000ft 198mph (315km/h); initial climb at sea level 1,800ft (548m)/min; service ceiling 26,700ft (8140m); take-off or landing over 50ft (15m) 1,500ft (480m); range with maximum cargo 298 miles (480km); range with maximum fuel and 2,303lb (1045kg) load 1,093 miles (1760km).
**Armament:** None normally fitted.
**History:** First flight 26 March 1971; pre-production aircraft 17 November 1972; service delivery 1973.
**Users:** Chile, Indonesia, Jordan, Nicaragua, Portugal, Saudi Arabia, Spain, Thailand, Turkey, Venezuela.

**Development:** Designed to replace the Ju 52/3m (T.2), DC-3 (T.3) and CASA 207 Azor (T.7) in the Spanish Air Force, the C.212 is designated T.12 in that service and has also been widely sold outside Spain. A simple unpressurized machine, it is intended as a 16-passenger transport, freighter (with full-section rear loading and air-dropping door), ambulance, photographic and survey aircraft and crew trainer. A civil version is also available. Deliveries began to No 461 Sqn at Gando (Las Palmas, Canary Is) and continued with 403 Sqn at Cuatro Vientos which has six photographic Aviocars. The Spanish AF is receiving eight pre-production and 32 production machines. Total orders exceed 100.

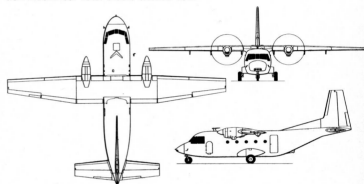

**Above: Three-view of C.212 (transport, photo, nav trainer similar).**

Above: In service with the Indonesian Air Force, this utility transport version of the Aviocar is designated T.12B; there is also the C.212B photo-survey version, designated appears to have been defeated by budgetary constraints, because proposed production was rejected in 1978 and 1979.

# Dassault Breguet Atlantic

## Br.1150 Atlantic

**Origin:** Design, Louis Breguet, France; manufacture, SECBAT multinational consortium.

**Type:** Maritime patrol and anti-submarine aircraft with normal crew of 12.

**Engines:** Two 6,106ehp Rolls-Royce Tyne 21 two-shaft turboprops.

**Dimensions:** Span 119ft 1in (36·3m); length 104ft 2in (31·75m); height 37ft 2in (11·33m).

**Weights:** Empty 52,900lb (24,000kg); maximum 95,900lb (43,500kg).

**Performance:** Maximum speed (above 16,400ft/5000m) 409mph (658km/h); patrol speed 199mph (320km/h); initial climb at gross weight 2,450ft (746m)/min; service ceiling 32,800ft (10,000m); patrol endurance 18 hours; maximum range 5,592miles (9000km).

**Armament:** Unpressurised weapon bay carries all NATO standard bombs, 385lb (175kg) depth charges, four homing torpedoes (or nine acoustic torpedoes) and HVAR rockets. Underwing racks for up to four AS.12, Martel or other missiles with nuclear or conventional warheads.

**History:** First flight 21 October 1961: (production aircraft) 19 July 1965; service delivery 10 December 1965.

**Users:** France (Aéronavale), W Germany (Marineflieger), Italy, Netherlands (Navy), Pakistan.

**Development:** The history of NATO shows the almost continual failure of its members to agree on weapon standardization, especially in aircraft. One of the few real attempts to do better was the 1958 decision to procure a standard aircraft to replace the Lockheed P-2. The French Br.1150 was selected from 25 designs submitted and in December 1959 two prototypes were ordered from NATO funds. Though most NATO members refused to have anything to do with it — often because their own design had not been

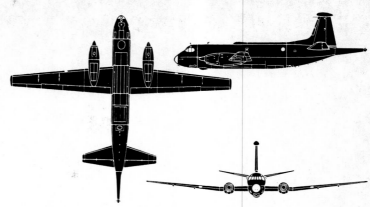

**Three-view of Br.1150 Atlantic (radome retracted).**

chosen — the programme was launched by France and Germany, which ordered 40 and 20 respectively. Subsequently the Netherlands Navy bought nine and the Italian Navy 18, so that finally the airframe was being built in all four countries, with avionics partly supplied from the USA and Britain. The engines were made by a British/Belgian/German/French/Italian consortium, with assembly by SNECMA of France. The Atlantic proved a most comfortable and efficient machine, with pressurization above the floor of the double-bubble fuselage and a great amount of room. The airframe is skinned mainly in metal honeycomb sandwich. Five of the German Atlantics carry special ECM systems. In 1979 two aircraft were being rebuilt as ANG (Atlantic new generation), for which the production line is to be reopened. The first of a planned 42 of these improved-sensor machines for France could be delivered in 1984.

**Below: Pleasing study of an Atlantic in its element. It belongs to 30° Stormo, Italian Marinavia, based at Cagliari.**

# Dassault Breguet Mirage F1

## Mirage F1.C

**Origin:** Avions Marcel Dassault/Breguet Aviation, France, in partnership with Aérospatiale, with Fairey and SABCA, Belgium, and CASA, Spain; licence production in S Africa managed by Armaments Development and Production Corporation.

**Type:** Single-seat multimission fighter.

**Engine:** (F1.C) 15,873lb (7200kg) thrust (maximum afterburner) SNECMA Atar 9K-50 single-shaft augmented turbojet; (F1.E) 18,740lb (8500kg) thrust (maximum afterburner) SNECMA M53-02 single-shaft augmented by-pass turbojet.

**Dimensions:** Span 27ft 6¾in (8·4m); length (F1.C) 49ft 2½in (15m); (F1.E) 50ft 11in (15.53m); height (F1.C) 14ft 9in (4·5m); (F1.E) 14ft 10½in (4.56m).

**Weights:** Empty (F1.C) 16,314lb (7400kg); (F1.E) 17,857lb (8100kg); loaded (clean) (F1.C) 24,030lb (10,900kg); (F1.E) 25,450lb (11,540kg); (maximum) (F1.C) 32,850lb (14,900kg); (F1.E) 33,510lb (15,200kg).

**Performance:** Maximum speed (clean, both versions) 915mph (1472km/h) (Mach 1·2) at sea level, 1,450mph (2335km/h) (Mach 2·2) at altitude (with modification to cockpit transparency and airframe leading edges F1.E capable of 2·5); rate of climb (sustained to Mach 2 at 33,000ft) (F1.C) 41,930–47,835ft (12,780–14,580m)/min; (F1.E) above 59,000ft (18,000m)/min; service ceiling (F1.C) 65,600ft (20,000m); (F1.E) 69,750ft (21,250m); range with maximum weapons (hi-lo-hi) (F1.C) 560 miles (900km); (F1.E) 621 miles (1000km); ferry range (F1.C) 2,050 miles (3300km); (F1.E) 2,340 miles (3765km).

**Armament:** (Both versions), two 30mm DEFA 5-53 cannon, each with 135 rounds; five Alkan universal stores pylons, rated at 4,500lb (2000kg) on centreline, 2,800lb (1350kg) inners and 1,100lb (500kg) outers; launch rails on tips rated at 280lb (120kg) for air-to-air missiles; total weapon load 8,820lb (4000kg). Typical air combat weapons, two Matra 550 Magic or Sidewinder on tips for close combat, one/two Matra 530 with infrared or radar homing, and one/two Matra Super 530 for long-range homing with large changes in height. Wide range of weapons for surface attack, plus optional reconnaissance pod containing cameras, SAT Cyclope infrared linescan and EMI side-looking radar.

**History:** First flight (F1-01) 23 December 1966; (pre-production F1-02) 20 March 1969; (production F1.C) 15 February 1973; (F1-M53, prototype for proposed F1.E) 22 December 1974; (F1.B trainer) 26 May 1976; service delivery (F1.C) 14 March 1973.

**Users:** Ecuador, Egypt, France, Greece, Iraq, Kuwait, Libya, Morocco, S Africa, Spain.

▶

**Three-view of the F1.C with Matra R 530s and Sidewinders.**

**Below: Cutaway drawing of the F1.C showing a representative selection of air-to-air missiles, six of which can be carried simultaneously.**

1 Dielectric tip
1 Dielectric tip antenna housings
2 Rear navigation light
3 IFF aerial
4 VHF 1 aerial
5 VOR/LOC aerial
6 Rudder upper hinge
7 Fin structure
8 UHF aerial
9 Main fin spar (machined)
10 Rudder control linkage
11 Rudder central hinge fairing
12 Rudder
13 Fin rear spar
14 VHF 2 aerial
15 Parachute release mechanism
16 Braking parachute
17 Variable nozzle
18 Cooling annulus
19 Pneumatic nozzle actuators
20 Jet pipe mounting link
21 Fuselage aft support frame (tailplane trunnion/fin rear spar)
22 Tailplane trunnion
23 Trunnion frame
24 Honeycomb-stabilized structure
25 Multi-spar box structure
26 Ventral fin (port and starboard)
27 Control input linkage
28 Tailplane power unit
29 Hydraulic lines
30 Fin rear spar attachment
31 Rudder trim actuator
32 Rudder power unit
33 Fin leading-edge structure
34 Port tailplane
35 main spar lower section
36 Spring rod
37 Servo control quadrant
38 Rudder pulley bellcranks and cables
39 Fin main spar
39 Fin main spar attachment
40 Fin root fittings
41 Sealed-sheath hydraulic line
42 Afterburner
43 Engine mounting rail
44 Chem-milled tank inner skin
45 Wing root fairing
46 Rear lateral fuselage fuel tanks
47 Engine mounting access panel
48 Control run access panel
49 Filler/cross-feed system (rear/forward lateral tanks)
50 Aileron linkage
51 Compressor bleed-air pre-cooler
52 Main wing/fuselage mounting frame
53 Machined wing skins
54 Inboard flap composite-honeycomb structure
55 Flap tracks
56 Perforated spoilers
57 Spoiler actuator
58 Wing tank fuel lines
59 Aileron trimjack
60 Aileron servo control
61 Aileron operating rod
62 Aileron inboard hinge
63 Port aileron
64 Aileron outboard hinge
65 Missile attachment points
66 Missile ignition box
67 Matra 550 Magic air-to-air missile
68 Missile adapter shoe
69 Hinged, powered leading-edge
70 Leading-edge actuation system
71 Pylon mount (outboard)
72 Pylon mount (inboard)
73 Port inboard weapon pylon

74 Matra 530 air-to-air missile (infra-red homing)
75 Inboard leading-edge actuator
76 Forged high-tensile steel root fitting
77 IFF aerial
78 Engine duct ventilation
79 Central fuselage fuel tank
80 Aileron control rod
81 Avionics bay
82 Electrical/hydraulic leads
83 Inverted-flight accumulator
84 Amplifier
85 Main radio/electronics bay
86 Water separator and air-conditioning turbo-compressor
87 Canopy hinge
88 Canopy actuating jack
89 Martin-Baker Mk 4 ejection seat
90 Clamshell jettisonable canopy
91 Gunsight
92 One-piece cast windshield frame
93 Instrument panel
94 Control column
95 Instrument panel shroud/gunsight mounting
96 Heated, bird-strike proof windshield
97 Pitot heads

98 Radar attachment points
99 Thomson-CSF Cyrano IV fire-control radar
100 Radar scanner
101 Glass-reinforced plastic radome
102 Tacan aerial
103 Front pressure bulkhead
104 Rudder pedals

105 Aileron control bellcrank
106 Control column base
107 Elevator control bellcrank
108 Retraction jack fairing
109 Nosewheel retraction jack
110 Oleo-pneumatic shock-absorber
111 Twin nosewheels
112 Nose gear forging
113 Guide link
114 Steering/centering jack
115 Nose gear door
116 Pilot's seat
117 Nose gear trunnion
118 Elevator linkage
119 Angled rear pressure bulkhead
120 Battery (24 volt)
121 Gun trough
122 Air intake shock-cone
123 Heat exchanger
124 Shock-cone electric motor

125 Boundary-layer bleed
126 Shock-cone guide track
127 Screw jack
128 Starboard air intake
129 DEFA cannon barrel
130 Auxiliary air intake door
131 Starboard airbrake
132 Starboard DEFA 30mm cannon
133 Forward fuselage integral fuel tank
134 Wing root fillet
135 Fuel pipes
136 Machined frame
137 Wing forward attachment point

138 Landing gear door actuator/linkage
139 Ammunition magazine (125 rounds)
140 Pre-closing landing gear door (lower)
141 Main landing gear well (starboard)
142 Main wing/fuselage

mounting frame
143 SNECMA Atar 9K50 turbojet (15,870 lb/7,200 kg with afterburner)
144 Main wing attachment
145 Machined frame
146 Wing rear attachment
147 Engine mounting trunnion
148 Inboard flap track

149 Flap actuator and linkage
150 Honeycomb trailing-edge structure
151 Double-slotted flaps
152 Perforated spoilers
153 Spoiler leading-edge piano hinge
154 Multi-spar integral tank structure

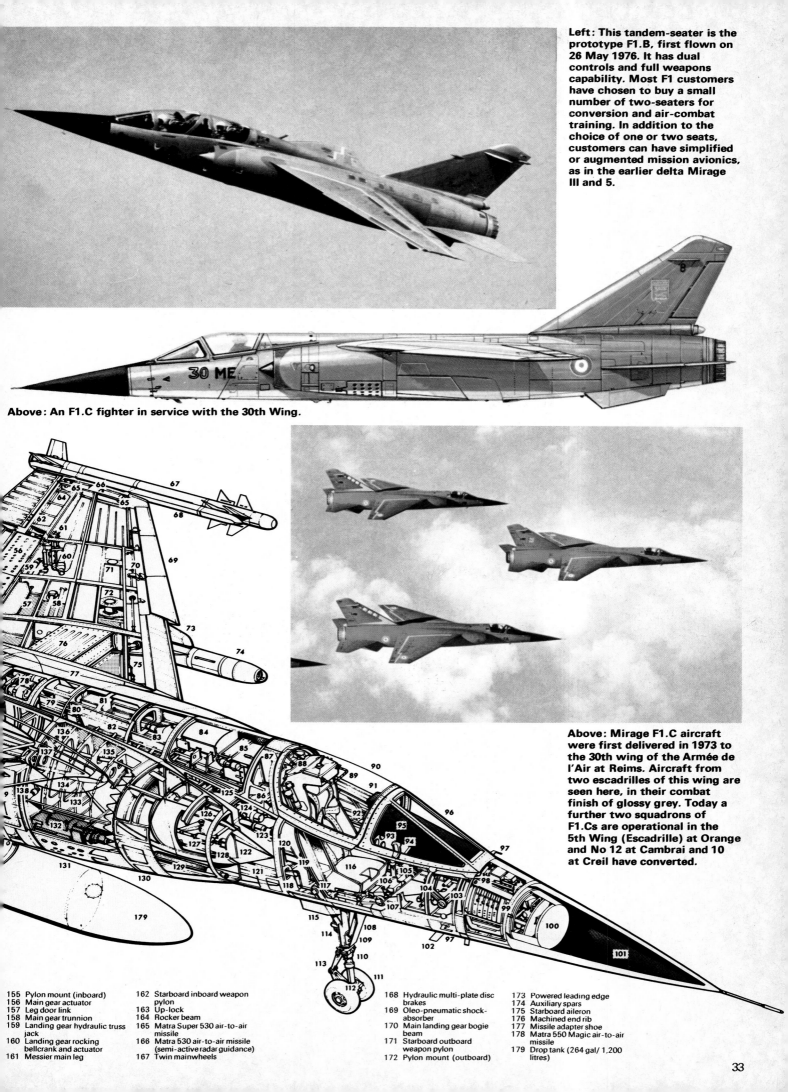

**Left:** This tandem-seater is the prototype F1.B, first flown on 26 May 1976. It has dual controls and full weapons capability. Most F1 customers have chosen to buy a small number of two-seaters for conversion and air-combat training. In addition to the choice of one or two seats, customers can have simplified or augmented mission avionics, as in the earlier delta Mirage III and 5.

**Above:** An F1.C fighter in service with the 30th Wing.

**Above:** Mirage F1.C aircraft were first delivered in 1973 to the 30th wing of the Armée de l'Air at Reims. Aircraft from two escadrilles of this wing are seen here, in their combat finish of glossy grey. Today a further two squadrons of F1.Cs are operational in the 5th Wing (Escadrille) at Orange and No 12 at Cambrai and 10 at Creil have converted.

155 Pylon mount (inboard)
156 Main gear actuator
157 Leg door link
158 Main gear trunnion
159 Landing gear hydraulic truss jack
160 Landing gear rocking bellcrank and actuator
161 Messier main leg

162 Starboard inboard weapon pylon
163 Up-lock
164 Rocker beam
165 Matra Super 530 air-to-air missile
166 Matra 530 air-to-air missile (semi-active radar guidance)
167 Twin mainwheels

168 Hydraulic multi-plate disc brakes
169 Oleo-pneumatic shock-absorber
170 Main landing gear bogie beam
171 Starboard outboard weapon pylon
172 Pylon mount (outboard)

173 Powered leading edge
174 Auxiliary spars
175 Starboard aileron
176 Machined end rib
177 Missile adapter shoe
178 Matra 550 Magic air-to-air missile
179 Drop tank (264 gal/ 1,200 litres)

33

▶**Development:** Recognising that the Mirage III family would eventually have to be replaced, the French government awarded Dassault a development contract for a successor in February 1964. This aircraft was the large Mirage F2, in the 20 ton (clean) class and powered by a TF306 turbofan engine. It broke away from the classic Mirage form in having a high-mounted conventional swept wing with efficient high-lift slats and flaps, used in conjunction with a slab tailplane. It flew on 12 June 1966. Dassault, however, had privately financed a smaller version of the F2, called F1, sized to be powered by a single Atar engine. This became increasingly attractive and effort was progressively transferred to it from the F2. It went supersonic on its fourth flight and, though it later crashed, the Armée de l'Air decided to buy 100 as replacements for the original Mirage IIIC interceptor and Vautour IIN. Thus was launched an aircraft which in most ways marks a tremendous advance on the tailless delta.

Thanks to the far higher efficiency of the new wing the field lengths and take-off and landing speeds are lower than for the delta Mirages, even though the weights are greater and the wing area much less. Increased thrust comes from the latest Atar engine and among the many less obvious advances are the Cyrano IV multi-mode radar and integral tankage for 45 per cent more fuel (trebling patrol endurance and doubling ground-attack mission radii). Combat manoeuvrability in many situations was increased by as much as 80 per cent and the all-round performance of the new fighter was outstanding. Sales to Israel were prohibited, but orders were soon placed by South Africa and Spain, the former also buying a manufacturing licence. More recently the F1 was chosen by several Middle East countries and many more sales seem certain.

In 1967 the French engine company, SNECMA, began the design of a completely new engine for the Super Mirage. To test the engine the F1 was an obvious choice, and the combination could not fail to be of interest in its own right. The M53 engine confers benefits in acceleration, climb, manoeuvrability and range and, to make up a more modern package, Dassault-Breguet proposed the fully modular Cyrano IV-100 radar and the SAGEM-Kearfott SKN 2603 inertial navigation system, as well as the SFENA 505 digital autopilot of the F1.C. The result is the F1.E, which from early 1974 was strongly, but unsuccessfully, pressed on overseas customers, particularly Belgium, the Netherlands, Denmark and Norway (which agreed a common objective in replacing their F-104Gs). The Armée de l'Air did not want the F1.E, but had agreed to buy a limited quantity had it been chosen by the four NATO nations. Two M53-powered prototypes were flown, but the M53-engined version was shelved in 1975. Today four versions are in production: (C) the basic aircraft, so far chosen by all customers; (E) the C with more advanced avionics (no longer offered with the M53 engine), chosen by Libya; (A) simplified avionics for low-level attack, for Libya and South Africa; (B) two-seater, for Kuwait and Libya.

**Top: The Ejercito del Aire (Spanish Air Force) calls the Mirage F1.C the C-14. The Spanish CASA company shares in some Dassault-Breguet manufacturing programmes.**
**Above: Another F1.C customer is the Hellenic (Greek) Air Force.**

# Dassault Breguet Mirage III and 5

## Mirage III and 5

**Origin:** Avions Marcel Dassault/Breguet Aviation, France (actual manufacture dispersed through European industry and certain models assembled in Belgium, Switzerland and Australia).
**Type:** Single-seat or two-seat interceptor, tactical strike, trainer or reconnaissance aircraft (depending on sub-type).
**Engine:** (IIIC) 13,225lb (6000kg) thrust (maximum afterburner) SNECMA Atar 9B single-shaft turbojet; (most other III and some 5) 13,670lb (6200kg) Atar 9C; (some III and 50) 15,873lb (7200kg) Atar 9K-50; (Kfir see separate entry).
**Dimensions:** Span 27ft (8·22m); length (IIIC) 50ft 10¼in (15·5m); (IIIB) 50ft 6¼in (15·4m), (5) 51ft (15·55m); height 13ft 11½in (4·25m).
**Weights:** Empty (IIIC) 13,570lb (6156kg); (IIIE) 15,540lb (7050kg); (IIIR) 14,550lb (6600kg); (IIIB) 13,820lb (6270kg); (5) 14,550lb (6600kg); loaded (IIIC) 19,700lb (8936kg); (IIIE, IIIR, 5) 29,760lb (13,500kg), (IIIB) 26,455lb (12,000kg).
**Performance:** Maximum speed (all models, clean) 863mph (1390km/h) (Mach 1·14) at sea level, 1,460mph (2350km/h) (Mach 2·2) at altitude; initial climb, over 16,400ft (5000m)/min (time to 36,090ft 11,000m, 3 min); service ceiling (Mach 1·8) 55,775ft (17,000m); range (clean) at altitude about 1,000 miles (1610km); combat radius in attack mission with bombs and tanks (mix not specified) 745 miles (1200km); ferry range with three external tanks 2,485 miles (4000km).
**Armament:** Two 30mm DEFA 5-52 cannon, each with 125 rounds (normally fitted to all versions except when IIIC carries rocket-boost pack); three 1,000lb (454kg) external pylons for bombs, missiles or tanks (Mirage 5, seven external pylons with maximum capacity of 9,260lb, 4200kg).
**History:** First flight (MD.550 Mirage I) 25 June 1955; (prototype Mirage III-001) 17 November 1956; (pre-production Mirage IIIA) 12 May 1958; (production IIIC) 9 October 1960; (IIIE) 5 April 1961; (IIIR) 31 October 1961; (IIIB) 19 July 1962; (Australian-assembled IIIO) 16 November 1963; (Swiss-assembled IIIS) 28 October 1965; (prototype 5) 19 May 1967; (Belgian-assembled 5BA) May 1970.
**Users:** (III) Abu Dhabi, Argentina, Australia, Brazil, Egypt, France, Israel, Lebanon, Libya, Pakistan, S Africa, Spain, Switzerland, Venezuela; (5) Abu Dhabi, Belgium, Colombia, Egypt, France, Gabon, Libya, Pakistan, Peru, Saudi Arabia, Venezuela, Zaire.

**Development:** The Mirage, which has come to symbolise modern aerial combat and to bring additional trade to France and incalculable prestige, especially in defence hardware, began in a most uncertain fashion. It was conceived in parallel with the Etendard II to meet the same Armée de l'Air light interceptor specification of 1952 and was likewise to be powered by two small turbojets (but, in this case, boosted by a liquid-propellant rocket engine in addition). As the small French engines were not ready, Dassault fitted the Mirage I with two British Viper turbojets and before the rocket was fitted this small delta was dived to Mach 1·15. With the rocket it reached Mach 1·3 in level flight. But Dassault had no faith in the concept of such low-power aircraft and after some work on the twin-Gabizo Mirage II took the plunge and produced a bigger and heavier Mirage III, powered by the 8,820lb thrust Atar 101G. From this stemmed the pre-production IIIA, with larger but thinner wing and completely redesigned fuselage housing the new Atar 9 engine. On 24 October 1958 Mirage IIIA-01 became the first West European aircraft to attain Mach 2 in level flight.

This clinched the decision of the Armée de l'Air to buy 100 of a slightly developed interceptor called Mirage IIIC, fitted either with guns or with a boost rocket for faster climb and better combat performance at heights up to 82,000ft. Normally the SEP 844 rocket was fitted to the IIIC, the sole armament being air-to-air missiles, such as Sidewinders and the big Matra R.530 used in conjunction with the CSF Cyrano radar, fitted to permit the new fighter to operate in all weather. Altogether 244 C models were delivered, large batches also going to South Africa and Israel (a nation which did much to develop and promote both the III and the 5). From the IIIC emerged the dual-control IIIB trainer, the longer and heavier IIIE for ground attack (with Marconi doppler radar for blind low-level navigation, new fire-control and navigation computer, and increased internal fuel) and the IIIR family of camera-equipped reconnaissance aircraft. By 1977 about 1,200 of the Mirage III family had been sold, including a fairly standard version made in Australia and an extremely non-standard version made in Switzerland after painful development problems which inflated the price and reduced the numbers bought.

In 1965 Israel suggested that Dassault should produce a special VFR (clear weather) version for ground attack in the Middle East, with the radar and fire control avionics removed and replaced by an extra 110 gallons of fuel and more bombs. The result was the Mirage 5 and Israel bought 50 of the first production batch of 60. It can be distinguished by its longer and much more pointed nose, devoid of radar unless the small Aida II is fitted. For political reasons the French refused to deliver the paid-for Mirages to Israel but more than 500 have been sold to many other countries and 106 were assembled, and partly constructed, in Belgium. Largely as a result of the French action, Israel developed its own improved version of the Mirage (see IAI Kfir, separate entry).

In addition to production aircraft there have been many experimental or unsold variants. One of the latter was the Spey-powered Mirage IIIW jointly proposed by Dassault and Boeing as a rival to the F-5 as a standard simple fighter for America's allies. Another non-starter was the Milan (Kite), fitted with retractable "moustache" foreplanes for shorter field-length and better manoeuvrability (this excellent idea is available on the Mirage 5). By far the biggest development programme concerned the enlarged and more powerful Mirage IIIV V/STOL fighter with a 19,840lb thrust SNECMA TF306 augmented turbofan for propulsion and eight 5,500lb thrust Rolls-Royce RB.162-31 lift jets. The IIIT was a non-VTOL of the same size and the equally large F2 led to the smaller (Atar-size) F1.

**Above: Not a Mirage delta with a tail but a pair of IIIO ground-attack fighters of the RAAF off the Australian coast.**

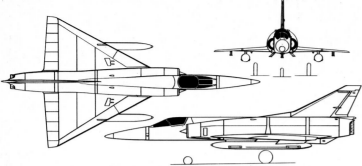

**Above: Three-view of Mirage 5, showing multi-sensor pods.**

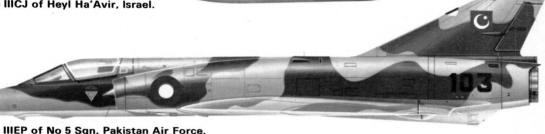

**Above: Mirage IIICJ of Heyl Ha'Avir, Israel.**

**Below: Most Mirage customers have bought dual-control trainer versions for pilot conversion to the speedy delta — with "back of the drag curve" characteristics — and weapon training. This is a Mirage 5-DV of Venezuela.**

**Above: Mirage IIIEP of No 5 Sqn, Pakistan Air Force.**

# Dassault Breguet Mirage IVA

## Mirage IVA

**Origin:** Avions Marcel Dassault/Breguet Aviation, France.
**Type:** Limited-range strategic bomber with crew of two.
**Engines:** Two 15,432lb (7000kg) thrust (maximum afterburner) SNECMA Atar 9K single-shaft augmented turbojets.
**Dimensions:** Span 38ft 10½in (11·85m); length 77ft 1in (23·5m); height 17ft 8½in (5·4m).
**Weights:** Empty 31,967lb (14,500kg); loaded 73,800lb (33,475kg).
**Performance:** Maximum speed (dash) 1,454mph (2340km/h) (Mach 2·2) at 40,000ft (13,125m), (sustained) 1,222mph (1966km/h) (Mach 1·7) at 60,000ft (19,685m); time to climb to 36,090ft (11,000m), 4min 15sec; service ceiling 65,620ft (20,000m); tactical radius (dash to target, hi-subsonic return) 770 miles (1240km); ferry range 2,485 miles (4000km).
**Armament:** No defensive armament other than ECM; one 60 kiloton freefall bomb recessed in underside of fuselage; alternatively, up to 16,000lb (7257kg) of weapons on hard points under wings and fuselage.
**History:** First flight (Mirage IV-001) 17 June 1959; (production IVA) 7 December 1963; first delivery 1964; final delivery March 1968.
**User:** France (Armée de l'Air CFAS).

**Development:** When the French government decided in 1954 to create a national nuclear deterrent force the most obvious problem was to choose a delivery system for the bombs. The likely enemy appeared to be the Soviet Union and this involved a long mission flown at high speed. After studying developments of the Vautour – a type used to form the nucleus of the *Force de Frappe* – Dassault began work on a bomber derived from a 1956 project for a twin-engined night fighter. After a year the design had to be scaled up to be powered by two Pratt & Whitney J75B engines, to meet more severe demands on speed, load and the range sufficient to reach desirable targets and then fly to places outside the Soviet Union. The final choice was to adopt extensive flight refuelling, which allowed the design to shrink again to an intermediate level. As a result the force of 62 bombers that was eventually created relies totally upon Boeing KC-135F tankers,

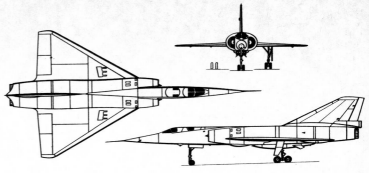

Above: Three-view of Mirage IVA showing bomb but not drop tanks.

with booms fitted for probe/drogue refuelling, and also upon the "buddy technique" whereby aircraft would fly a mission in pairs, one carrying a bomb and the other spare fuel and a refuelling hose-reel for transfer to its partner. Even so, the initial planning of the Commandement des Forces Aériennes Stratégique presupposed that most missions would be one-way (or at least would not return to France). Dispersal has been maximised, with the force divided into three Escadres (91 at Mont de Marsan, 93 at Istres and 94 at Avord), which in turn are subdivided into three four-aircraft groups, two of which are always dispersed away from Escadrille HQ. Despite being a heavy and "hot" aircraft, the IVA has also been rocket-blasted out of short unpaved strips hardened by quick-setting chemicals sprayed on the soil. Of the original total of 62 about 51 remain operational, 36 being at readiness as noted above and the remainder in reserve. They will be used only for reconnaissance after 1985, following conversion of the first 12 aircraft in 1978–80.

**Below: Practice takeoff by a Mirage IVA of 93e Escadre using ATO rockets. This technique is used to allow the bombers to be dispersed to otherwise unusable short airfields.**

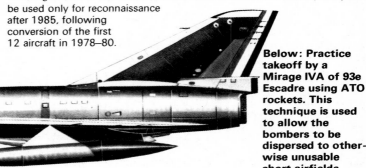

Above: Mirage IVA with tanks; some are now camouflaged.

# Dassault Breguet Mirage 2000

## Mirage 2000 (single- and two-seat versions)

**Origin:** Avions Marcel Dassault/Breguet Aviation, France.
**Type:** Multi-role fighter with emphasis on interception and air superiority combat.
**Engine:** One SNECMA M53-5 single-shaft afterburning by-pass turbojet (low-ratio turbofan) with maximum thrust of 12,350lb (5602kg) dry and 19,840lb (9000kg) with afterburner.
**Dimensions:** Span 29ft 6in (9·0m); length 50ft 3½in (15·33m).
**Weights:** Empty, not released; normal takeoff, air-intercept mission 33,000lb (14,969kg).
**Performance:** Maximum speed at 36,000ft (11,000m) Mach 2·3, 1,518mph (2440km/h).
**Armament:** Two 30mm DEFA 5-53 cannon; normal air-intercept load two Matra Super 530 and two Matra 550 Magic air-to-air missiles; intention is to develop ground-attack version with maximum overload of 11,025lb (5000kg) of weapons and/or tanks and ECM pods on five external hardpoints.
**History:** Announcement of project December 1975; first flight 10 March 1978; production delivery, probably late 1982.
**Users:** Egypt (intended licence-production), France.
**Development:** In December 1975 the French government cancelled the Dassault-Breguet Super Mirage, which had been publicised as the Avion de Combat Futur and mainstay of the Armée de l'Air in the 1980s. In its place it announced a decision to award a study contract with Marcel Dassault for a smaller and simpler single-engined delta fighter outwardly looking very much like the Mirage III of 20 years earlier. In fact the Mirage 2000 — sometimes called the Delta 2000 — will differ significantly from the old Mirage, in aerodynamics, propulsion, structure and equipment. Aerodynamically it will be designed to incorporate American discoveries in CCV (control-configured vehicle) technology, in which aircraft are deliberately made unstable — for example, by positioning the centre of gravity much further back than usual — and using high-authority fail-safe flight-control systems to keep them under control. The result is either a smaller wing or, as in the Mirage 2000, dramatically higher manoeuvrability. Unlike the earlier Mirage deltas the 2000 will have leading-edge devices, either hinged droops or some form of slats, which will work in conjunction with the trailing-edge elevons to counteract the unstable pitching moment, or, in a tight turn, relax their effort or even help the aircraft to pitch nose-up. In the landing configuration the leading-edge devices (the French call it a "variable-camber" wing) will allow the elevons to be deflected down, adding to lift, whereas in earlier tailless deltas they have to be deflected up, effectively adding to weight just at the worst time.

Already the Mirage 2000 is being publicised as "being able to outclass combat aircraft presently being developed and produced in the Western world". It will have: "fly-by-wire" multi-channel electrically signalled flight controls; composite materials, carbon fibre being mentioned; large-radius Karman fairings (a reference to area ruling of the fuselage for minimum transonic drag); an elaborate weapon system with "g.p." (general-purpose?) computer and inertial unit; and long-range digital radar. Ratio of thrust to weight is to exceed unity. Such features are what one would expect of such an aircraft, but the problems are clearly enormous, especially in a time of severe inflation and economic pressures. France has since 1975 made attempts to acquire the base of technology, especially in digital avionics, necessary to build the Mirage 2000, but has little capability as yet. Only a single French aircraft, a two-seat Mirage IIIB with Sfena system, has flown with a primitive fly-by-wire system. Thomson-CSF estimate it will take "seven to eight years" to develop a 170-km-range digital radar needed to match the developed Super 530 missile. France has little experience of advanced composite structures, and that only in small test pieces and heli-copters. SNECMA has not announced how the M53 engine, with very limited flight-time and no other application, is going to be increased in thrust by 35 per cent. If the aircraft to fly in 1978 is truly a prototype, and not the first off a production line, it will need everything to go right to meet an in-service date of 1982 with a developed aircraft. Not least, the proposed price of Fr40 to 50 million (£4·5 to 5·5 million) will be extremely difficult to hold, even in December 1975 Francs, because the magnitude of the system-development problems to France appear to have been grossly under-estimated.

In the original announcement the Mirage 2000 was described as "limited to high-speed and high-level interception and reconnaissance. . . . Attack and penetration at low levels will be undertaken by a different type." (The cancelled Super Mirage had been intended to fulfil all tactical roles.) But in December 1976 the Chief of Staff of the Armée de l'Air said he personally considered it would be necessary to build an interdictor and reconnaissance (he implied at low level) version of the Mirage 2000. It became known at this time that the new delta will apparently have nine weapon stations, which is diametrically opposed to the uncompromised high-altitude dog-fight concept announced in December 1975; and low-level use is dia-metrically opposed to a large-area delta. The Armée de l'Air has from the start hoped to buy 200 Mirage 2000s, twice the number it judged it could afford of the Super Mirage. But future progress of the programme, helped by US industry strictly on an inter-company rather than a government basis, will be instructive to watch.

## Dassault Breguet Super Mirage 4000

**Type:** Multi-role combat aircraft.
**Engines:** (prototype) two SNECMA M53-5 single-shaft afterburning by-pass turbojets each with maximum thrust of 19,840lb (9000kg).
**Armament:** Not fitted to prototype.
**History:** Company launch January 1976; first flight 9 March 1979.
**User:** None announced (August 1979).

Aerodynamically the 4000 closely resembles a scale-up (about ×1·25) of the 2000, but with a proportionally larger fin and the important addition of electrically signalled powered canards on the inlets in place of the smaller fighter's fixed strakes. The radar is the completely new RDM (Radar Doppler Multifonction) Cyrano 500, tested in a Vautour and also intended for export models of Mirage 2000. An I-band track-while-scan set, it is a frequency-agile pulse-Doppler with several functions unavailable in the RDI (Radar Doppler Impulsions) of the regular 2000.

In January 1976 Marcel Dassault announced that, as a private venture, he was launching the Delta Super Mirage as a long-range multi-role aircraft for export. One hesitates to doubt the credibility of either the man or the company, but to fund such a programme would need many times the net worth of the company, and no consortium of overseas buyers (South Africans? Arabs? Black Africans?) appears to be conceivable. It would not be im-possible for the company to finish the defunct tailed Super Mirage prototype, which was to have flown in July 1976, as an empty shell to show possible customers what the proposed Delta Super Mirage would look like. To develop it as an operational aircraft does not by any stretch of the imagination appear possible. One is left to conclude that M Dassault either expects the French government to find the money, which is extremely unlikely, or he hopes to organise a programme involving a large number of nations pre-pared to share the costs and risks.

**Below: Dassault's Mirage 2000 and 4000 are remarkable achievements, funded by the company and the French government. Here 2000 prototypes 01 (white) and 03 (camouflaged) are seen escorting the big twin-engined 4000, whose power-driven canards are an important new feature. The intention is to build a production 4000 with the proposed M88 engine, a new radar and many other items which are stretching the French budget.**

# Dassault Breguet
# Super Etendard

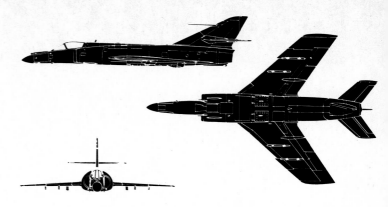

## Super Etendard

**Origin:** Avions Marcel Dassault/Breguet Aviation, France.
**Type:** Single-seat carrier strike fighter.
**Engine:** 11,265lb (5110kg) thrust SNECMA Atar 8K-50 single-shaft turbojet.
**Dimensions:** Span 31ft 5¾in (9·6m); length 46ft 11½in (14·31m); height 12ft 8in (3·85m).
**Weights:** Empty 13,889lb (6300kg); loaded 25,350lb (11,500kg).
**Performance:** Maximum speed 745mph (1200km/h) at sea level, Mach 1 at altitude; initial climb 24,600ft (7500m)/min; service ceiling 52,495ft (16,000m); range (clean) at altitude, over 1,243 miles (2000km).
**Armament:** Two 30mm DEFA cannon; mission load up to 9,921lb (4500kg) carried on five pylons.
**History:** First flight (converted Etendard) 28 October 1974; first delivery, late 1977.
**User:** France (Aéronavale).

**Development:** During the late 1960s it had been expected that the original force of Etendards would be replaced, in about 1971, by a specially developed version of the Jaguar, the M version with single main wheels, full carrier equipment and specially fitted for the naval strike role. A Jaguar M completed flight development and carrier compatability, but for various reasons, mainly concerned with politics and cost, this was rejected by the Aéronavale and a search began for an alternative. After studying the A-4 Skyhawk and A-7 Corsair, the Aéronavale chose Dassault-Breguet's proposal for an improved Etendard. This has a substantially redesigned structure, for operation at higher indicated airspeeds and higher weights; a new and more efficient engine, obtained by removing the afterburner from the Atar 9K-50 of the Mirage F1.C; completely new inertial navigation

**Three-view of the Super Etendard (centreline pylon not shown).**

system, produced mainly by SAGEM with American help; new multi-mode nose radar, produced jointly by Thomson-CSF and Electronique Marcel Dassault, with especially good performance in surface vessel detection and attack; and much greater and more varied mission load. Flight development was completed in 1974-77 with three converted Etendard IVs, the first testing the engine, the second the avionics and weapons, and the third the new wing with slats and double-slotted flaps like the Jaguar. In 1973 the Aéronavale announced it would buy 100, but this has now been cut back to 30, and service delivery delayed until late 1978.

**Below: Portrait of the first Super Etendard development aircraft, externally almost indistinguishable from the production version. This aircraft was fitted with most of the operational equipment, including the SAGEM (Singer-Kearfott) inertial navigation system and the Thomson-CSF/EMD Agave radar. Though called a "strike fighter", in fact the Super Etendard is a tactical attack machine for low-level use.**

# Dassault Breguet/Dornier Alpha Jet

## Alpha Jet

**Origin:** Jointly Dassault/Breguet, France, and Dornier GmbH, W Germany, with assembly at each company.
**Type:** Two-seat trainer and light strike/reconnaissance aircraft.
**Engines:** Two 2,976lb (1350kg) thrust SNECMA/Turboméca Larzac 04 two-shaft turbofans.
**Dimensions:** Span 29ft 11in (9·12m); length (excluding any probe) 40ft 3¾in (12·29m); height 13ft 9in (4·2m).
**Weights:** Empty 6,944lb (3150kg); loaded (clean) 9,920lb (4500kg), (maximum) 15,432lb (7000kg).
**Performance:** (clean) maximum speed 576mph (927km/h) at sea level, 560mph (900km/h) (Mach 0·85) at altitude; climb to 39,370ft (12,000m), less than 10 minutes; service ceiling 45,930ft (14,000m); typical mission endurance 2hr 30min; ferry range with two external tanks 1,510 miles (2430km).
**Armament:** Optional for weapon training or combat missions, detachable belly fairing housing one 30mm DEFA or 27mm Mauser cannon, with 125 rounds, or two 0·50in Brownings, each with 250 rounds; same centreline hardpoint and either one or two under each wing (to maximum of five) can be provided with pylons for maximum external load of 4,850lb (2200kg), made up of tanks, weapons, reconnaissance pod, ECM or other devices.
**History:** First flight 26 October 1973; first production delivery originally to be early 1976, actually late 1978.
**Users:** Belgium, Cameroun, France, W Germany, Ivory Coast, Nigeria, Togo.

**Development:** Realisation that the Jaguar was too capable and costly to be a standard basic trainer led to the Armée de l'Air issuing a requirement for a new trainer in 1967. The chosen design was to be capable of use in the light ground attack role, in which the Luftwaffe had a parallel need for an aircraft. On 22 July 1969 the two governments agreed to a common specification and to adopt a common type of aircraft produced jointly by the two national industries. After evaluation against the Aérospatiale (Nord)/MBB E650 Eurotrainer, the Alpha Jet was selected on 24 July 1970. Aircraft for the two partners are nearly identical. France makes the fuselage and centre section and Germany the rear fuselage, tail and outer wings. SABCA of Belgium makes minor portions. Engines, originally shared by two French companies (see above), are being produced in partnership with MTU and KHD of Germany, plus a small share by FN of Belgium. Trainer aircraft are assembled at Toulouse (France) and attack versions at Oberpfaffenhofen (Germany). Decision to go ahead with production was reached on 26 March 1975. It was expected at that time that France and Germany would each buy 200, and that Belgium would buy 33, but the programme has slipped by more than two years, resulting in increased costs. In 1979 full production was achieved.

**Above: Unfortunately the most colourful Alpha Jet, the 04 prototype, was lost in a crash in 1976, but this was not due to a fault in the aircraft.**

**Above: Three-view of Alpha Jet prototype with armament.**

**Below: The Luftwaffe Alpha Jet 1A is equipped as a light attack machine, with reconnaissance capability. The first of 175 was delivered to Fürstenfeldbruck (JaboG 49) in 1979.**

# MBB BO 105

## 105C and 105VBH

**Origin:** Messerschmitt-Bölkow-Blohm, Munich, West Germany; licence production by PADC, Philippines.
**Type:** Multi-role all-weather helicopter.
**Engines:** Two 400shp Allison 250-C20 turboshafts.
**Dimensions:** Diameter of four-blade main rotor 32ft 2¾in (9·82m); length overall (rotors turning) 38ft 10¾in (11·84m); height overall 9ft 9½in (2·98m).
**Weights:** Empty 2,469lb (1120kg) (with tactical armament about 2,645lb, 1200kg); maximum loaded 5,070lb (2300kg).
**Performance:** Maximum speed S/L 167mph (270km/h); max cruise 144mph (232km/h); max climb 1,378ft (420m)/min; range with standard fuel, no reserve (S/L) 363 miles (585km).
**Armament:** Various options including six Hot or TOW missiles and stabilised sight system.
**History:** First flight 16 February 1967; type certification October 1970.
**Users:** (Military) W Germany, Netherlands, Nigeria, Philippines.

**Development:** Using an advanced rotor developed with Aérospatiale, this small twin-turbine helicopter is expensive but extremely capable, and is fully aerobatic and cleared for IFR operation in the most adverse conditions. By 1977 some 350 had been sold, including a small number for military use. The German Army has evaluated the 105VBH liaison and observation version, and an anti-tank 105 with six Hots and all-weather sight system. An order for about 300 had long been expected for the German Army when this book went to press, and several other military sales were being negotiated. Boeing Vertol sell in the Americas and PADC assemble the basic 105C in the Philippines. The BO 106 is a wider version, seating seven instead of four.

**Right: Launch of a HOT missile from the No 4 tube of a BO 105 equipped with only four tubes.**

**Below: The standard six-tube HOT installation, with the head of the stabilized sight projecting above the cabin.**

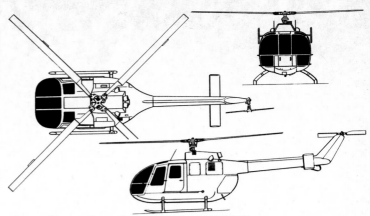

**Above: Three-view of the wide-body BO 106.**

# Panavia Tornado IDS

## Tornado IDS (GR.1)

**Origin:** Panavia Aircraft GmbH, international company formed by British Aerospace, MBB of West Germany and Aeritalia.

**Type:** Two-seat multirole combat aircraft optimised for strike.

**Engines:** Two Turbo-Union RB.119 Mk 101 or 103 augmented turbofans, each rated at 15,800lb (7,167kg) or over 16,000lb (7,258kg) thrust with full afterburner.

**Dimensions:** Span (25°) 45ft 7½in (13·90m), (65°) 28ft 2½in (8·60m); length 54ft 9½in (16·7m); height 18ft 8½in (5·70m).

**Weights:** Empty equipped 31,065lb (14,091kg); loaded (clean) about 45,000lb (20,411kg); maximum loaded about 60,000lb (27,200kg)

**Performance:** Maximum speed (clean) over 920mph (1,480km/h, Mach 1·2) at sea level, over 1,452mph (2,337km/h, Mach 2·2) at altitude; service ceiling over 50,000ft (15,240m); combat radius with 8,000lb (3,629kg) bombload (hi-lo-hi) 863 miles (1,390km).

**Armament:** Two 27mm Mauser cannon in lower forward fuselage; seven pylons, three tandem on body and four on swinging wings, for external load up to 18,000lb (8,156kg).

**History:** First flight (prototype) 14 August 1974, (production IDS) July 1979, service delivery (IDS to trials unit) February 1978, squadron service (RAF, Luftwaffe, Marineflieger) 1982.

**Users:** West Germany (Luftwaffe, Marineflieger), Italy, UK (RAF).

**Development:** Most important military aircraft in Western Europe, the Tornado was the outcome of the first multinational collaborative programme to embrace design and development as well as manufacture, and to lead to a completely successful exercise in both management and hardware. Though from the start a multirole aircraft, the Tornado IDS (interdiction strike) is optimised for the long-range all-weather blind first-pass attack mission against the most heavily defended surface targets, including ships, it is by far the most capable aircraft of its size ever built, and not least of its achievements is that on typical missions its fuel burn is roughly equal to that of an F-16, 60 per cent that of an F-4 and about 50 per cent that of an F-15 or Su-24, while carrying at least as heavy and varied a load as the best of those aircraft. Features include a Texas Instruments multimode forward-looking radar with the option of various types of programmable software, a terrain-following radar, electrically

signalled fly-by-wire flight controls with artificial stability, fully variable supersonic inlets (which help make this the fastest aircraft in the world at low level, and one of the fastest at all heights, despite the extremely compact lightweight engines), advanced avionic systems to manage the array of stores that can be carried (which exceeds that of any other aircraft), and modern tandem cockpits with head-up and head-down display in the front and three electronic displays in the back. Among the stores which have been cleared are all tactical bombs of the four initial customers, nine rocket pods, Sidewinder AAMs, and Sea Eagle, Kormoran, Maverick, Alarm. GBU-15, Paveway, AS.30 and AS.30L, Martel (seldom to be carried), Aspide, BL.755, JP.233 and MW-1; Harpoon and possibly other cruise missiles may be added. All aircraft have two guns, Martin-Baker Mk 10 automatic zero/zero seats, a gas-turbine APU which is self-cooling and can be left running on the ground, automatically scheduled lift-dumpers, anti-skid brakes and (as a further option) a braking parachute. There is provision, so far exercised only by the RAF, to bolt on a flight-refuelling probe package above the right side below the canopy. All sub-types have very comprehensive EW systems, with advanced RHAWS and either the Elettronica EL/73 deception jammer and ELT 553 ECM pod, or Marconi Avionics Sky Shadow. Deliveries began in 1980 to the TTTE (Tornado Trinational Training Establishment), located at RAF Cottesmore in England. This had a strength of 50 aircraft, a high proportion being dual-pilot trainers for pilot conversion, the rest being for training navigators and complete crews. Aircraft from all three nations were used, the crews likewise being completely multinational until they paired up for final training as teams. By 1982 two further major training establishments were operational, that for the Luftwaffe (WaKo) being at Erding and for the RAF (TWCU) at Honington. RAF squadrons began with Nos 9 (Honington) and 617 (Marham), followed by eight in RAF Germany: 15 and 16 (ex-Buccaneer) at Laarbruch, all four squadrons in the former Jaguar wing at Brüggen, No 9 (from Honington) and, in 1986, equipment of No 2(II) Sqn with aircraft specially configured for reconnaissance. Marineflieger MFG 1 and 2 are both converted from the F-104G, while the Luftwaffe is converting four JaboG wings, Nos 31-34. Italy's AMI is using 54 aircraft to replace the F/RF-104G in the 28°, 132° and 154° gruppi, with further aircraft equipping the 3° GEV (maintenance/training squadron) at Cameri. Total national commitments, all delivered or in process of manufacture by 1984, comprise: RAF 219 with designation GR.1 (plus a pre-production machine brought up to GR.1 standard); Marineflieger 112; Luftwaffe 212; and AMI 99 plus some pre-production aircraft updated. This gives a total of 664, of which 355 had been delivered by 1984.

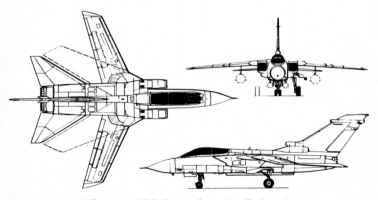

**Three-view of Tornado IDS (interdictor/strike) variant.**

**Right: Three Tornados of the Trinational Training Establishment in Italian, British and German markings. Crews from the three countries were completely multinational until the final pairings were made.**

**Below: Shock diamonds glow in the jets thrusting aloft the first Italian-assembled Tornado, prototype 05. This first flew at Turin Caselle in December 1975, but was subsequently damaged in a heavy landing.**

Left: Four 1,000lb (454kg) low-drag bombs fall from the fuselage pylons of Tornado 02 during the first weapon trials in 1975.

**Above: 02 Tornado development prototype with "tri-national" markings.**

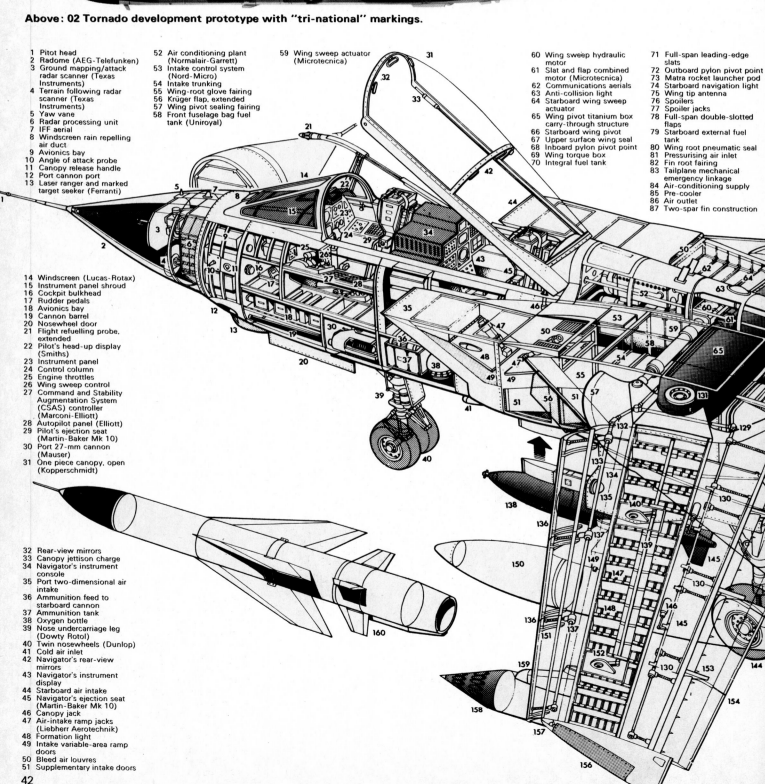

1 Pitot head
2 Radome (AEG-Telefunken)
3 Ground mapping/attack radar scanner (Texas Instruments)
4 Terrain following radar scanner (Texas Instruments)
5 Yaw vane
6 Radar processing unit
7 IFF aerial
8 Windscreen rain repelling air duct
9 Avionics bay
10 Angle of attack probe
11 Canopy release handle
12 Port cannon port
13 Laser ranger and marked target seeker (Ferranti)

14 Windscreen (Lucas-Rotax)
15 Instrument panel shroud
16 Cockpit bulkhead
17 Rudder pedals
18 Avionics bay
19 Cannon barrel
20 Nosewheel door
21 Flight refuelling probe, extended
22 Pilot's head-up display (Smiths)
23 Instrument panel
24 Control column
25 Engine throttles
26 Wing sweep control
27 Command and Stability Augmentation System (CSAS) controller (Marconi-Elliott)
28 Autopilot panel (Elliott)
29 Pilot's ejection seat (Martin-Baker Mk 10)
30 Port 27-mm cannon (Mauser)
31 One piece canopy, open (Kopperschmidt)

32 Rear-view mirrors
33 Canopy jettison charge
34 Navigator's instrument console
35 Port two-dimensional air intake
36 Ammunition feed to starboard cannon
37 Ammunition tank
38 Oxygen bottle
39 Nose undercarriage leg (Dowty Rotol)
40 Twin nosewheels (Dunlop)
41 Cold air inlet
42 Navigator's rear-view mirrors
43 Navigator's instrument display
44 Starboard air intake
45 Navigator's ejection seat (Martin-Baker Mk 10)
46 Canopy jack
47 Air-intake ramp jacks (Liebherr Aerotechnik)
48 Formation light
49 Intake variable-area ramp doors
50 Bleed air louvres
51 Supplementary intake doors

52 Air conditioning plant (Normalair-Garrett)
53 Intake control system (Nord-Micro)
54 Intake trunking
55 Wing-root glove fairing
56 Krüger flap, extended
57 Wing pivot sealing fairing
58 Front fuselage bag fuel tank (Uniroyal)

59 Wing sweep actuator (Microtecnica)

60 Wing sweep hydraulic motor
61 Slat and flap combined motor (Microtecnica)
62 Communications aerials
63 Anti-collision light
64 Starboard wing sweep actuator
65 Wing pivot titanium box carry-through structure
66 Starboard wing pivot
67 Upper surface wing seal
68 Inboard pylon pivot point
69 Wing torque box
70 Integral fuel tank

71 Full-span leading-edge slats
72 Outboard pylon pivot point
73 Matra rocket launcher pod
74 Starboard navigation light
75 Wing tip antenna
76 Spoilers
77 Spoiler jacks
78 Full-span double-slotted flaps
79 Starboard external fuel tank
80 Wing root pneumatic seal
81 Pressurising air inlet
82 Fin root fairing
83 Tailplane mechanical emergency linkage
84 Air-conditioning supply
85 Pre-cooler
86 Air outlet
87 Two-spar fin construction

**Above: The second (04) and third (07) German-assembled Tornadoes flying from Manching with MBB crews. The second is carrying a large store on the right-hand body pylon.**

**Above: Prototype 06, flown by BAC at Warton in December 1975, was the first Tornado to carry the internal armament of two 27mm IKWA-Mauser cannon. Here it has supersonic drop tanks.**

88 Communications antenna
89 Passive ECM housing
90 Electronic tuning controls
91 Fin tip antenna
92 Tail warning radar (Elettronica)
93 Tail navigation light
94 Rudder
95 Starboard taileron surface
96 Thrust-reverser bucket-doors, open
97 Starboard fully-variable exhaust nozzle
98 Rear spine end fairing
99 Port fully variable exhaust nozzle
100 Thrust-reverser bucket-door, closed
101 Bucket-door actuator
102 Nozzle actuator
103 Rear spine

104 Port taileron construction
105 Taileron tip fairing
106 Runway arrester hook (Nardi)
107 Taileron actuating link
108 Taileron pivot
109 Port taileron actuator (Fairey Hydraulics)
110 Turbo-Union RB. 199-34R-2 engine
111 Airbrake jack
112 Port airbrake, extended
113 Vortex generators
114 Rudder actuator (Fairey Hydraulics)

115 Airbrake hinge point
116 Fly-by-wire tailplane control unit
117 Engine access doors
118 Intake frame
119 APU (KHD) in starboard gearbox bay
120 Rear fuselage bag fuel tank (Uniroyal)
121 Intake ducting

122 Hydraulic reservoir
123 Hydraulic system accumulator (Dowty)
124 Engine drive auxiliary gearbox (KHD)
125 Wing-housing cross frame
126 Wing-root pneumatic seal
127 Undercarriage frame
128 Main undercarriage retraction jack
129 Flap control shaft

130 Flap screw jacks
131 Port wing pivot bearing
132 Drive shaft gearbox
133 Leading-edge slat drive shaft
134 Main undercarriage door
135 Landing lamp
136 Full-span leading-edge slats, extended
137 Slat control units
138 1,000lb bomb (454kg)
139 Pylon pivot control rod
140 Inboard pylon pivot point
141 Main undercarriage leg (Dowty Rotol)
142 Fuselage bomb rack

143 Wing swept position
144 Port mainwheel (Dunlop)
145 Spoilers
146 Spoiler jack (Fairey Hydraulics)
147 Wing box construction
148 Integral fuel tank
149 Port inboard pylon
150 Port external fuel tank
151 Leading-edge slat rails
152 Outboard pylon pivot point
153 Flap track rail
154 Full-span double-slotted flaps, extended
155 Line of wing sweep
156 Wing tip antenna
157 Port navigation light
158 Matra rocket launcher
159 Port outboard pylon
160 MBB Jumbo air-to-surface missile (cancelled)

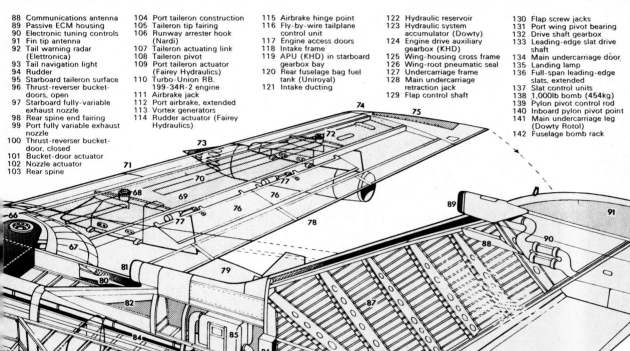

The cutaway drawing is remarkably complete, bearing in mind the fact that most of the equipment and system details of even the IDS Tornado are subject to security restrictions. The MBB Jumbo missile is, in fact, unlikely to be developed, but Tornado still has to be cleared to carry a wider range of stores and equipment than any other combat aircraft in history. By the spring of 1977 nearly all weapon trials had been completed except for the extreme upper end of the flight envelope which had been held back by unavailability of full-thrust engines—a problem now overcome.

# Panavia Tornado ADV

## Tornado ADV (F.2)

**Origin:** Panavia Aircraft GmbH, and especially British Aerospace.
**Type:** Long-range all-weather interceptor.
**Engines:** Two Turbo-Union RB.199 Mk 104 augmented turbofans, each rated at more than 16,000lb (7,258kg) thrust in full afterburner.
**Dimensions:** Span (25°) 45ft 7¼in (13·90m), (67°) 28ft 2½in (8.60m); length 59ft 3in (18.06m); height 18ft 8½in (5.70m).
**Weights:** Empty equipped about 31,500lb (14,290kg); clean takeoff (maximum internal fuel) 47,500lb (21,546kg).
**Performance:** Maximum speed (clean) about 1,500mph (2,414km/h, Mach 2·27) at altitude; combat mission with maximum AAM load, 2hr 20min on station at distance of 375 miles (600km) from base with allowance for combat.
**Armament:** One 27mm Mauser cannon; four Sky Flash (later AMRAAM) recessed under fuselage and two AIM-9L Sidewinder (later ASRAAM) AAMs.
**History:** First flight 27 October 1979; service delivery late 1984; operational squadron late 1985.
**User:** UK (RAF).

**Development:** Though it is purely a British development, the ADV (air-defence variant) of Tornado is produced by the same tri-national airframe and engine groupings as are the IDS series, and in due course it is likely to become the most widely used model, with greater export interest from more countries. It is unquestionably the most efficient long-range interceptor in the world, outperforming all known rivals in almost all respects (an exception is the sheer straight-line speed of the MiG-25 and -31), with engines of amazingly small size and low fuel burn. Designated Tornado F.2 by the RAF, the interceptor has about 80 per cent commonality with the original IDS aircraft, and most of the airframe and aircraft systems are unchanged. The forward fuselage, made by BAe in any case, is completely new. This contains: a new pair of cockpits, with later electronic displays, different symbology, greater processing and storage capacity and a wet-film HDD recorder; Marconi/Ferranti AI.24 Foxhunter FMICW radar, with multimode lookup/lookdown TWS and missile guidance capability; deletion of one of the two guns; installation of a permanent flight-refuelling probe, fully retractable on the left side; installation of a ram-air turbine giving full hydraulic system power at high altitudes with main engines inoperative, down to below 230mph (370km/h); and addition of the Cossor 3500 series IFF, Singer ECM-resistant data link (with Nimrod AEW.3, for example, or ground stations) and a second INS. Other airframe changes include forward extension of the fixed wing gloves, giving a major change in lift and agility, provision of 200gal (909lit) of extra fuel in the extended fuselage, and belly recesses for four Sky Flash (later AIM-120A) medium-range missiles, with twin-ram cartridge-powered ejection giving clean launch at maximum negative g. The engines have various upratings which at high speeds and altitudes become large and significant, with extended jetpipes which improve afterbody shape and reduce drag; they also have digital control. The only item not mentioned in connection with the production F.2 is the magnifying optical VAS (visual augmentation system) for positive identification of aircraft at great distances, which was regarded as a crucial item early in the programme. By mid-1984 British Aerospace had almost completed the basic flight development programme with the three

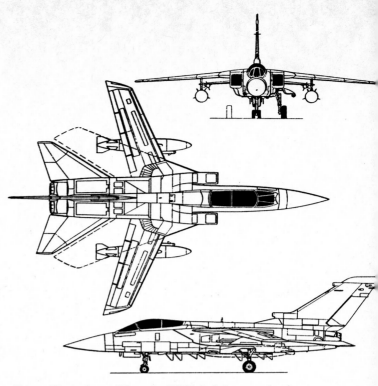

**Above: Three view of Tornado ADV (air defence variant).**

prototypes, and had delivered the first two production aircraft. The latter are both ATs (dual pilot ADV trainers), which after a spell at Boscombe Down cleared fully operational F.2s to form the OCU (Operational Conversion Unit) at Coningsby in September 1984. The first production batch of 15 were complete by this time, temporarily fitted with Mk 103 engines. The second and third RAF batches, numbering 52 and 92 aircraft, have the Mk 104 from the outset, as well as automatic schedule wing-sweep and manoeuvre device (wing slats and flaps at 25° to 45× sweep) to give enhanced manoeuvrability with minimal pilot workload. Updates planned for the future include still more powerful engines, even larger (495gal, 2,250lit) drop tanks, the AIM-120A (AMRAAM) and ASRAAM missiles and further improvements to the avionics. All-round performance has been demonstrated as equal to or even better than predicted, with acceleration remaining "healthy" at Mach 2, and 800 knots (912mph, 1,483km/h) indicated airspeed being registered at medium altitudes (true speed being much greater and at heights down to 2,000ft (610m). few if any other fighters are capable of this. From early 1985 the Tornado F.2 will begin to take its place in the RAF protecting the UK Air Defence Region. It will equip seven squadrons, the first five being at Leuchars (two) and Leeming (three).

**Above:** The additional length of the Tornado ADV is readily apparent in this photograph of the first prototype. Although the ADV has about 80 per cent commonality with the IDS variant, the forward fuselage is completely new, and as well as the redesigned cockpits it houses a versatile multi-mode Foxhunter AI.24 radar and a permanent, fully retractable flight-refuelling probe. Only one gun is carried, and other new equipment includes a ram-air turbine for emergency power, new IFF and data link equipment and a second inertial navigation system.

**Left:** The first prototype of the Tornado ADV, developed specifically for the RAF and designated F.2 in service, banks over the Blackpool, Lancashire, seafront. Among the many impressive attributes of this outstanding new fighter are a demonstrated time on combat air patrol of 2hr 20min at a distance of 375 miles (600km) from base without inflight-refuelling, and performance in terms of speed at both high and low altitudes is unlikely to be exceeded by any other fighter.

**Right:** As well as the lengthened nose to accommodate the new radar, the Tornado ADV's fuselage was stretched slightly aft of the cockpit to allow two pairs of Sky Flash air-to-air missiles to be carried in tandem. Completing the normal weapon load are the internal 27mm cannon and AIM-9 Sidewinders carried on the fuel tank pylons, while future plans include the replacement of the Sky Flash missiles by the improved launch-and-leave AIM-120 AMRAAM, and the use of ASRAAM short-range missiles in place of the AIM-9Ls currently carried by the F.2.

# Saab 105

## SK 60A, B and C, Saab 105O and 105G

**Origin:** Saab-Scania, Linköping, Sweden.
**Type:** Trainer and multi-role tactical aircraft.
**Engines:** (SK 60) two 1,640lb (743kg) thrust Turboméca Aubisque geared turbofans; (others) two 2,850lb (1293kg) General Electric J85-17B single-shaft turbojets.
**Dimensions:** Span 31ft 2in (9·50m); length (SK 60) 34ft 5in, (others) 35ft 5¼in (10·80m); height 8ft 10in (2·70m).
**Weights:** Empty (SK 60) 5,534lb (2510kg), (G) 6,757lb (3065kg); maximum loaded (SK 60) 8,380lb (3800kg) aerobatic or 8,930lb (4050kg) other, (G) 14,330lb (6500kg).
**Performance:** Maximum speed (clean, low level) (SK 60 at 8,820lb) 447mph (720km/h), (G) 603mph (970km/h); initial climb (SK 60) 3,440ft (1050m)/min, (G) 11,155ft (3400m)/min; service ceiling (SK 60) 39,370ft (12,000m), (G) 42,650ft (13,000m); max range, high altitude on internal fuel (SK 60) 1,106 miles (1780km), (G) 1,230 miles (1980km).
**Armament:** Wing stressed for six hardpoints to carry total external load of (SK 60) 1,543lb (700kg), (G) 5,180lb (2350kg) including gun pods to 30mm calibre, 1,000lb bombs, missiles, tanks and target gear.
**History:** First flight 29 June 1963, (production SK 60A) 27 August 1965, (G) 26 May 1972.
**Users:** Austria, Sweden.

**Above: It has long been Flygvapen policy to disperse combat units to straight public highways. These four SK 60Cs from F20 at Uppsala have recce noses and full weapons capability.**

**Development:** Developed as a private venture, a rare thing for Saab, this neat side-by-side trainer and multi-role aircraft has hydraulically boosted elevators and ailerons, ejection seats replaceable by four fixed seats for liaison duties, and a wide range of avionics and weapon options. The 150 SK 60s of the Royal Swedish AF comprise A (basic trainers), B (weapon training and strike) and C (reconnaissance) sub-types. Austria uses the 105O. The G has airframe modifications, heavier and more varied weapon loads and a precision nav/attack system.

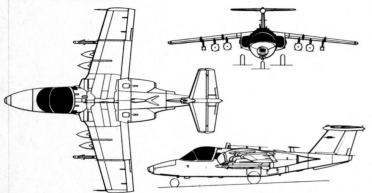

**Above: Three-view of basic SK 60A, with Sidewinders.**

**Below: Another multi-role Saab 105 wing is F21 at Lulea. Many of their aircraft are SK 60C models, but this formation is of the basic series without reconnaissance cameras in the nose.**

# Saab 35 Draken

## J35A, B, D and F, Sk35C, S35E and export versions

**Origin:** Saab-Scania AB, Linköping, Sweden.
**Type:** (J35) single-seat all-weather fighter-bomber; (Sk35) dual trainer; (S35) single-seat all-weather reconnaissance.
**Engine:** One Svenska Flygmotor RM6 (licence-built Rolls-Royce Avon with SFA afterburner): (A, B, C) 15,000lb (6804kg) RM6B; (D, E, F and export) 17,110lb (7761kg) RM6C.
**Dimensions:** Span 30ft 10in (9·4m); length 50ft 4in (15·4m) (S35E, 52ft); height 12ft 9in (3·9m).
**Weights:** Empty (D) 16,017lb; (F) 18,180lb (8250kg); maximum loaded (A) 18,200lb; (D) 22,663lb; (F) 27,050lb (12,270kg); (F-35) 35,275lb (16,000kg).
**Performance:** Maximum speed (D onwards, clean) 1,320mph (2125km/h, Mach 2·0), (with two drop tanks and two 1,000lb bombs) 924mph (1487 km/h, Mach 1·4); initial climb (D onwards, clean) 34,450ft (10,500m)/min; service ceiling (D onwards, clean) about 65,000ft (20,000m); range (internal fuel plus external weapons, typical) 800 miles (1300km), (maximum fuel) 2,020 miles (3250km).
**Armament:** (A) two 30mm Aden M/55 in wings, four Rb 324 (Side-winder) missiles; (B) as A plus attack ordnance to maximum of 2,200lb (1000kg); (C) none; (D) as B; (E) usually none but provision as A; (F) one 30mm Aden plus two Rb27 Falcon (radar) and two Rb28 Falcon (infra-red) missiles, plus two or four Rb324; (F-35) two 30mm Aden plus nine stores pylons each rated at 1,000lb (454kg) all usable simultaneously, plus four Rb324.
**History:** First flight 25 October 1955; (production J35A) 15 February 1958; final delivery (35XS) 1975, (Danish TF-35) 1976.
**Users:** Denmark, Finland, Sweden (RSAF).

**Development:** Again in advance of any other country in Western Europe, the Saab 35 was designed in 1949–51 as an all-weather supersonic fighter able to use small airfields. Erik Bratt and his team arrived at the unique "double delta" shape after studying different ways of packaging the fuel and equipment, the best arrangement being with items one behind the other

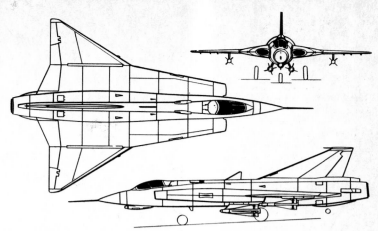

Above: Three-view of the Falcon-armed J35F ("Filip" to the Swedish Air Force).

giving a long aircraft of very small frontal area. In 1960 attack wing F13 found the A (Adam) simple to fly and maintain, sensitive in pitch and yet virtually unbreakable. B (Bertil) was more complex, with S7 collision-course fire control integrated with the Swedish Stril 60 air defence environment. Most Sk35C trainers were converted Adams. D (David) was first to reach Mach 2, despite continual increases in weight mainly due to fuel capacity raised from 493 to 680 gallons. E (Erik) carries French OMERA cameras and in 1973 was updated with external British Vinten night/low-level pods. F (Filip) is an automatic interceptor with Ericsson (Hughes basis) radar of pulse-doppler type. Production was closed at 606 with 40 multi-role F-35/RF-35/TF-35 aircraft for Denmark and 12 XS for Finland assembled by Valmet Oy.

Above: J35A ("Adam" to the Swedish AF).

**Below:** A pleasing study of one of the six TF-35XD multi-role tandem-seat Drakens of the Royal Danish Air Force. Denmark also uses the most capable of all Draken variants, the single-seat 35XD, and the RF-35 with the Red Baron night reconnaissance pod.

# Saab 37 Viggen

## AJ37, JA37, SF37, SH37 and Sk37

**Origin:** Saab-Scania AB, Linköping, Sweden.
**Type:** (AJ) single-seat all-weather attack; (JA) all-weather fighter; (SF) armed photo-reconnaissance; (SH) armed sea surveillance; (SK) dual trainer.
**Engine:** One Svenska Flygmotor RM8 (licence-built Pratt & Whitney JT8D two-shaft turbofan redesigned in Sweden for Mach 2 and fitted with SFA afterburner); (AJ, SF, SH and Sk) 25,970lb (11,790kg) RM8A; (JA) 28,086lb (12,750kg) RM8B.
**Dimensions:** Span of main wing 34ft 9½in (10·6m); length (AJ) 53ft 5¾in (16·3m); (JA37 with probe) 53ft 11in; height 18ft 4½in (5·6m).
**Weights:** Not disclosed, except AJ37 "normal armament" gross weight of 35,275lb (16,000kg).
**Performance:** Maximum speed (clean) about 1,320mph (2135km/h, Mach 2), or Mach 1·1 at sea level; initial climb, about 40,000ft (12,200m)/min (time from start of take-off run to 32,800ft–10,000m = 100sec); service ceiling, over 60,000ft (18,300m); tactical radius with external stores (not drop tanks), hi-lo-hi profile, over 620 miles (1000km).
**Armament:** Seven pylons (option: nine) for aggregate external load of 13,200lb (6000kg), including Rb04E or Rb05A missiles for attack, and Rb27, Rb28 and Rb324 missiles for defence. In addition the JA37 has a 30mm Oerlikon KCA gun and will carry "new long- and short-range missiles for air-to-air interception"; Skyflash is being evaluated.
**History:** First flight 8 February 1967; (production AJ) 23 February 1971; service delivery (AJ) June 1971.
**User:** Sweden (RSAF).

**Development:** Yet again blazing a trail ahead of other nations, the Royal Swedish Air Board planned System 37 in 1958–61 as a standardized weapon system to be integrated with the Stril 60 air-defence environment of radars, computers and displays. Included in the system is a standard platform (in this case a supersonic manned aircraft) produced in five versions each tailored to a specific task. Thanks to a unique configuration with a 400 sq ft wing preceded by a canard foreplane with trailing-edge flaps, the Viggen (Thunderbolt) has outstanding STOL (short take-off and landing) performance and excellent turn radius at all speeds. Efficient and prolonged operations are possible from narrow strips 500m (1,640ft) in length, such as stretches of highway. Equipment in all versions includes headup display, autothrottle/speed control on approach, no-flare landing autopilot and thrust reverser. The AJ operates camouflaged in attack wings F7, F15 and F6, with production continuing in 1977 on a mix of AJ, SF, SH and Sk models. At the beginning of the year about 145 had been delivered of the total orders for 180 of these versions. During 1976 Viggens in RSAF service were grounded until the cause of inflight structural (wing) failures

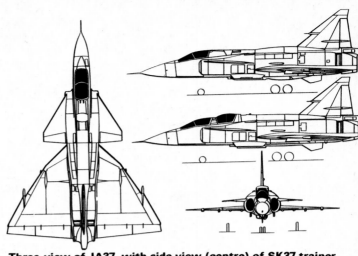

**Three-view of JA37, with side view (centre) of SK37 trainer.**

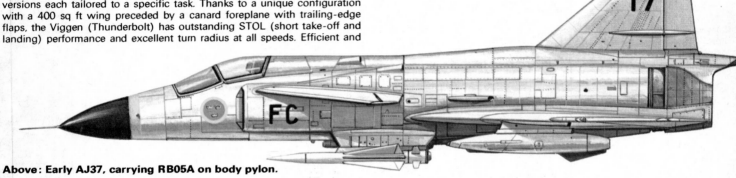

**Above: Early AJ37, carrying RB05A on body pylon.**

1 Dielectric radome
2 Planar-array scanner
3 Ericsson PS-01 pulse-doppler radar
4 Avionics bay
5 Radar/avionics cooling air
6 Nosewheel doors
7 Twin nosewheels (forward retracting)
8 Nosewheel leg
9 Control runs
10 Nosewheel leg pivot point
11 Rudder pedal
12 Canopy frame (with windshield de-icing)
13 Control column
14 Head-up display shroud
15 Starboard console (weapons, avionics)
16 Weapons/gunsight
17 Windshield
18 Canopy
19 Starboard intake
20 Headrest
21 Ejection seat
22 Port engine intake
23 Inlet duct
24 Forward (canard) wing/fuselage attachment points
25 Main fuselage fuel tank
26 Canopy hinges
27 Starboard forward (canard) wing
28 Canard flaps
29 Intakes
30 Radio equipment bay
31 Engine oil coolers (centre and starboard tanks)
32 Electric generator drive

33 Centre fuselage avionics pack
34 Port avionics bay
35 Hydraulics tank
36 Forward (canard) wing structure
37 Honeycomb flap construction
38 Ram-air turbine
39 Aircraft gearbox
40 Starter
41 Oxygen cylinder
42 Central computer and avionics
43 Engine intake
44 Fuselage saddle fuel tank (forward wall) (see 52)
45 Cabin air outlet
46 Cooling package
47 Engine forward attachment point
48 Fuel lines
49 Volvo Flygmotor RM 8 turbofan (25,970 lb/11,790 kg with afterburner)
— cooler (port tank)
50 Aircraft gearbox cooler
51 Main wing attachment point
52 Fuselage saddle fuel tank (rear wall) (see 44)
53 Air brake
54 Engine aft attachment point
55 Control runs
56 Fin front spar/fuselage attachment point
57 Starboard integral fuel tank
58 Starboard ECM bullet
59 Starboard outer elevon actuator
60 Starboard elevon (outer section)
61 Fin structure
62 VHF aerial
63 Rudder honeycomb construction

64 Rudder
65 Rudder actuator fairing
66 Actuator support
67 Fin rear spar/fuselage attachment point
68 Control linkage
69 Afterburner
70 Reverser clamshells
71 Rear navigation light
72 Tail fairing
73 Primary nozzle
74 Port elevon (inner section)
75 Elevon actuator (inner)

76 Rear spar
77 Elevon actuator (centre)
78 Port elevon (outer section)
79 Honeycomb construction
80 Elevon actuator (outer)
81 Outer leading-edge structure
82 Port ECM bullet
83 Port integral fuel tank
84 Main spar

85 Undercarriage door (inner)
86 Wheel well
87 Mainwheel leg pivot point
88 Inner leading-edge structure
89 Mainwheel leg (Motala)
90 Mainwheel leg door (outer)
91 Mainwheel scissors
92 Tandem mainwheels

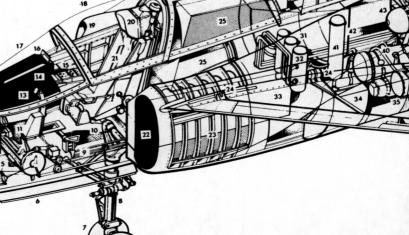

**Above:** Though departure of an AJ37 is marked by extreme noise and fuel consumption, this unique tandem-delta aircraft offers great advantages. It is especially outstanding in radar and weapon-delivery systems, turn radius with heavy ordnance load, and short no-flare landing with thrust-reverser.

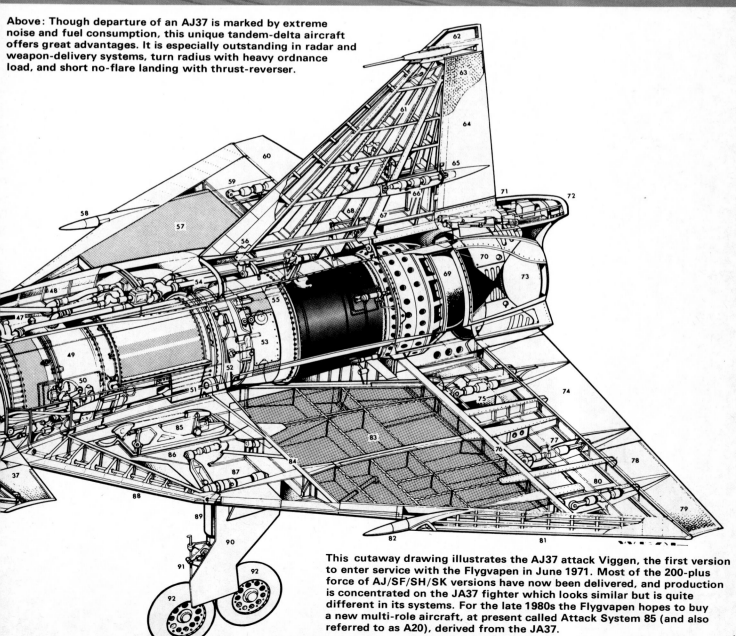

This cutaway drawing illustrates the AJ37 attack Viggen, the first version to enter service with the Flygvapen in June 1971. Most of the 200-plus force of AJ/SF/SH/SK versions have now been delivered, and production is concentrated on the JA37 fighter which looks similar but is quite different in its systems. For the late 1980s the Flygvapen hopes to buy a new multi-role aircraft, at present called Attack System 85 (and also referred to as A20), derived from the JA37.

►had been fully explained and aircraft rectified. Apart from this the Viggen has proved as outstanding as it looked on paper in the 1960s, and even today no other Western European aircraft can rival it for radar performance, flight performance and short field length in all weathers. The latest Viggen variant, the JA37, is considerably different, with a new engine, very powerful gun, UAP 1023 pulse-doppler radar, digital automatic flight control system and extremely advanced inertial measurement and central computer systems. The development effort for the JA37 rivals that for the complete original aircraft, but with the help of a fleet of special-purpose test aircraft (some new and most rebuilds of early AJ and other models) the JA was cleared for production in 1976. By the start of 1977 most of the initial batch of 30 were on the line, and service delivery is due in 1978. Eventually 200 are to equip eight squadrons.

**Right: A tandem-seat SK37 of F15 wing at Soderhamm taxies out for a training sortie. This replaces the fuselage fuel tank and electronics by a rear cockpit, with Saab-Scania rocket-assisted seat, bulged canopy and twin periscopes. To counter the extra side area the fin has increased height and area. This dual-control version can fly attack missions with any AJ37 weapons.**

**Below: An AJ37 with some of the more common external stores. The largest is the centreline fuel tank. In the front row are low-drag bombs with stand-off fuzes. In the second row are (from the outside) RB28 Falcon air/air missile; RB05A air/surface missile (now being supplemented by RB05B with long TV seeker nose); two types of store apparently carrying multi-sensor reconnaissance equipment; two types of launcher for Bofors 135mm rockets; and RB324 Sidewinder air/air missiles. Under the wings are large RB04E anti-ship missiles.**

# SEPECAT Jaguar

## Jaguar GR.1 and T.2, Jaguar A and E, and Jaguar International

**Origin:** SEPECAT, consortium formed by British Aerospace (BAC) and Dassault-Breguet, France.

**Type:** (GR.1, A and International (I.)) single-seat all-weather attack; (T.2 and E) dual operational trainer.

**Engines:** Two Rolls-Royce/Turboméca Adour two-shaft augmented turbofans: (except I.) 7,305lb (3313kg) Adour 102; (I.) 8,000lb (3630kg) Adour 804.

**Dimensions:** Span 28ft 6in (8·69m); length (except T.2, E) 50ft 11in (15·52m); (T.2, E) 53ft 11in (16·42m); height 16ft 1½in (4·92m).

**Weights:** Empty, classified but about 15,000lb (6800kg); "normal take-off" (ie, internal fuel and some external ordnance) 23,000lb (10,430kg); maximum loaded 34,000lb (15,500kg).

**Performance:** Maximum speed (lo, some external stores) 820mph (1320km/h, Mach 1·1), (hi, some external stores) 1,055mph (1700km/h, Mach 1·6); climb and ceiling, classified; attack radius, no external fuel, hi-lo-hi with bombs, 507 miles (815km); ferry range 2,614 miles (4210km).

**Armament:** (A, E) two 30mm DEFA 553 each with 150 rounds; five pylons for total external load of 10,000lb (4536kg); (GR.1) as above but guns two 30mm Aden; (T.2) as above but single Aden. (International) wide range of options including increased external loads.

**History:** First flight (E) 8 September 1968; (production E) 2 November 1971; (production GR.1) 11 October 1972; squadron delivery (E, A) May 1972, (GR, T) June 1973.

**Users:** Ecuador, France, India, Oman, UK (RAF).

**Development:** Developed jointly by BAC in Britain and Dassault-Breguet in France, to meet a joint requirement of the Armée de l'Air and RAF, the Jaguar is a far more powerful and effective aircraft than originally planned and has already demonstrated unmatched capabilities in service. The ▶

Above: Takeoff of a prototype E-type trainer in France in 1969, with "dual-nationality" markings. All 40 of this simple training version have now been delivered to the Armée de l'Air, the main units being the 7th wing at St Dizier and 11th at Toul.

Above: Close formation fly-past by Jaguar A-type attack aircraft and E-type trainers of the 7e wing. The Armée de l'Air deliberately bought simpler Jaguars than the RAF, though they are now being updated by optional laser and/or radar equipment.

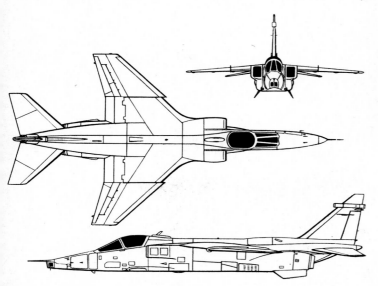

Above: Three-view of Jaguar GR.1 without stores.

Below: A dramatic firing picture of a Matra 550 Magic air-to-air dogfight missile being loosed from an overwing pylon. The aircraft was a BAC-modified Jaguar International, with uprated Adour 804 engines, trials with which were very successfully completed in 1976.

► original idea was a light trainer and close-support machine, with 1,300lb weapon load, but with British pressure this was upgraded to today's outstanding aircraft whose only marketing problem is the fact that the French partner prefers aircraft which appear to be all-French (yet, in fact, Dassault makes only the same proportion of the Mirage F1 as it does of the Jaguar, namely, about 50 per cent). Despite this unhappy political scene the sheer merit of the Jaguar, and the enthusiastic missionary work done by its operating units in the Armée de l'Air and RAF, is gradually winning valuable orders, beginning with Ecuador and Oman in 1974. Further sales are likely with the more powerful International version now flying. The two basic single-seat versions share a common airframe but are totally different in equipment. The French A model has a simple twin-gyro platform, doppler, and a basic navigation computer; in 1977 an Atlis laser pod was being added. The RAF GR.1 has inertial navigation, head-up display, projected map display, radar height, integrated nav/attack system and laser ranger, as well as comprehensive ECM and option of a multi-sensor reconnaissance pod. All versions can have nose radar, refuelling probe and the option of overwing pylons for light dogfight missiles (Jaguar development aircraft have flown with Matra Magics in these positions). Thanks to a dynamic programme of engine development Jaguar users have the option of various increased-thrust Adours, including the Mk 804 (Adour 26) fitted to the basic Jaguar International, and the even more powerful Adour 56 and 58 (in the 10,000lb, 4500kg class) which will be available from 1980. It is the intention of the RAF to select one of the uprated engines and convert all Jaguar engines to this standard, to gain even better field length and flight performance with large mission loads. By 1977 some 300 aircraft had been delivered, and several new customers were engaged in contract negotiation.

Above: A Jaguar GR.1 of No 2 (written II) Sqn, RAF Laarbruch, tries out its multi-sensor reconnaissance pod over the German countryside.

Above: Jaguar A tactical version of Armée de l'Air.

1 Pitot head
2 Pitot probe
3 'Chisel nose' with glass windows
4 Ferranti laser ranger and target marker
5 Air data computer
6 Waveform generator
7 Two total-pressure probes
8 Radio altimeter
9 HF/VHF power amplifier
10 Equipment bay cooling ducts
11 Intake
12 Nav/attack electronics compartments
13 External emergency canopy release
14 Ajax feel unit (pitch control)
15 Nosewheel well
16 Instrument panel
17 Projected map display (head-down)
18 Windscreen
19 Head-up display panel
20 Upward-hinged canopy
21 Martin-Baker Mk 9 zero-zero ejector seat
22 Honeycomb cockpit side panels
23 Instrument console
24 Access panels
25 Cannon barrel
26 Battery and electrics bay
27 Intake

28 Spring-loaded auxiliary inlet doors
29 30mm Aden cannon
30 Main undercarriage side door
31 Undercarriage retraction jack
32 Integrally-stiffened frame
33 Ammunition trough
34 Duct bolt-up joints
35 Inlet duct frames
36 Duct/fuselage attachment plate
37 Cold-air unit
38 Ram-air intake
39 Twin VHF homer aerials
40 Inner dorsal spine (hydraulic and cable runs)
41 Slat motor and gearbox
42 Drop tank (264 gal/1,200 litres)
43 Starboard inner pylon
44 1000 lb (454 kg) bomb
45 Starboard outer stores pylon
46 Leading-edge steel slat-rail
47 Starboard navigation light
48 Honeycomb-filled spoiler
49 Wing fence
50 Pylon mount
51 Fuel lines
52 Wing construction
53 Starboard wing integral fuel tank
54 Dorsal anti-collision beacon
55 Control rods
56 Wing centre-joint
57 Forward wing-fixing joint
58 Box-section centre-keel
59 Ram-air intake
60 Honeycomb-filled flap
61 Primary heat-exchanger
62 Upper fuselage access panels
63 Engine forward mounting point
64 Accumulator No 2 system

65 Hydraulic system pressure reservoir No 2
66 Air extractor duct
67 Upper fuselage access panels
68 Inward/outward vent valve
69 Starboard tailplane
70 Fin construction
71 Magnetic detector
72 Built-up leading edge
73 Passive ECM sensor fairing
74 VHF/UHF aerial
76 Rear navigation light
77 HF aerial
78 Honeycomb-filled rudder
79 Fuel dump vent
80 Braking parachute housing
81 Rudder power control unit
82 Control run linkage
83 Tailplane control units
84 Tailplane pivot point
85 Tailplane construction

86 Tailplane discontinuity (inboard rear portion higher)
87 Honeycomb-filled outer section
88 Arrester hook (extended)
89 Variable nozzle flaps
90 Afterburner
91 Aft fuselage integral fuel tanks
92 Engine aft mounting point
93 Rolls-Royce/Turboméca Adour 102 turbofans (7,305 lb/3,313 kg thrust with maximum afterburner)
94 Centre fuselage section
95 Air brake actuator
96 Air brake (extended)
97 Wing fence
98 Pylon mount
99 Full-span trailing-edge double-slotted flaps
100 Port navigation light
101 1,000 lb (454 kg) bomb
102 Port outer stores pylon
103 Leading-edge slat
104 Port inner stores pylon
105 Drop tank (264 gal/1,200 litres)
106 Low-pressure twin main-

wheel tyres
107 Shock-absorber strut
108 Mainwheel leg
109 Drag strut
110 Undercarriage flap
111 Centreline ventral stores pylon (shown lowered)
112 Tandem BL 755 cluster bombs
113 Cannon port
114 Nosewheel

Above: Agave radar combined with Ferranti laser ranger, an option for Jaguar International.

115 Single (starboard) axle fork
116 Nosewheel leg
117 Two landing lights (one 450W, one 250W)
118 Nosewheel door
119 Anti-shimmy gear
120 Towing lug

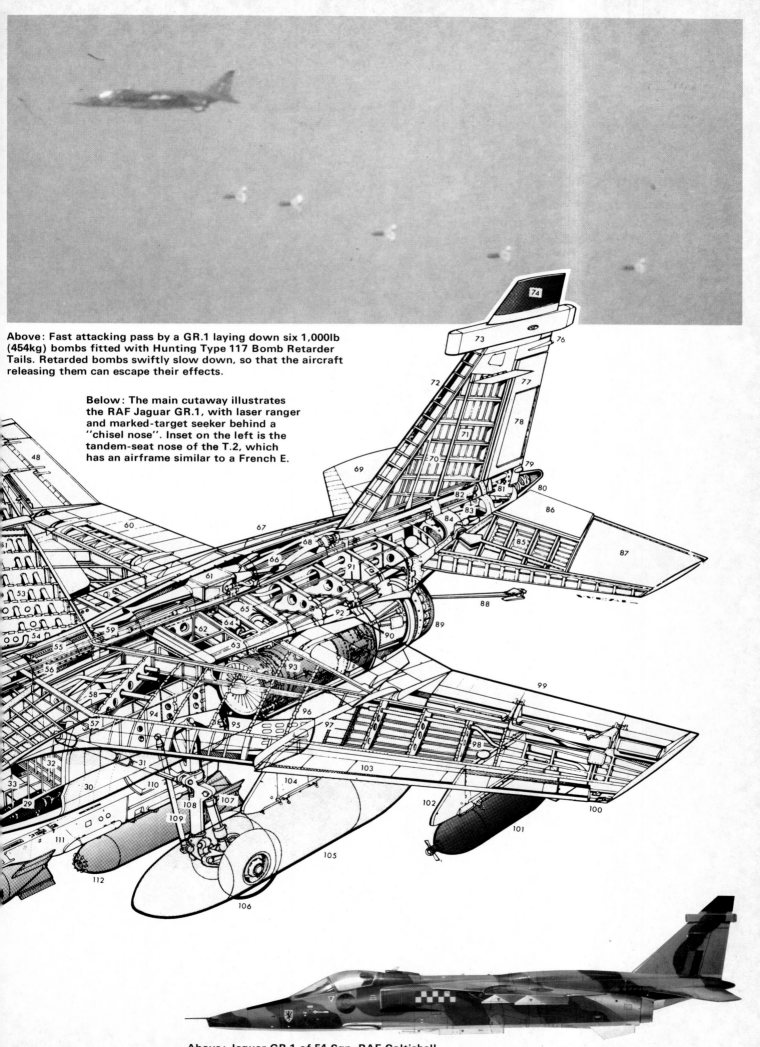

Above: Fast attacking pass by a GR.1 laying down six 1,000lb (454kg) bombs fitted with Hunting Type 117 Bomb Retarder Tails. Retarded bombs swiftly slow down, so that the aircraft releasing them can escape their effects.

Below: The main cutaway illustrates the RAF Jaguar GR.1, with laser ranger and marked-target seeker behind a "chisel nose". Inset on the left is the tandem-seat nose of the T.2, which has an airframe similar to a French E.

Above: Jaguar GR.1 of 54 Sqn, RAF Coltishall.

# SIAI-Marchetti SF.260

## SF.260M, W and SW

**Origin:** SIAI-Marchetti SpA, Varese, Italy.
**Type:** (M) trainer, (W) tactical multi-role, (SW) surveillance.
**Engine:** One 260hp Avco Lycoming O-540-E4A5 flat-six.
**Dimensions:** Span 27ft 4¾in (8·35m); length 23ft 3½in (7·10m); height 7ft 11in (2·41m).
**Weights:** Empty (M, equipped) 1,664lb (755kg); maximum loaded 2,645lb (1200kg).
**Performance:** (M at max wt) maximum speed 211mph (340km/h); initial climb 1,496ft (456m)/min; service ceiling 16,400ft (5000m); take-off or landing over 50ft (15m) within 2,543ft (775m); range with max fuel 925 miles (1490km) (SW, about 1,400 miles, 2250km).
**Armament:** (W) one underwing hardpoint on each side rated at 330lb (150kg) for Matra 7·62mm gun pods, 120kg bombs or wide range of other stores.
**History:** First flight (MX) 10 October 1970, (W) May 1972.
**Users:** Belgium (M), Burma (M), Dubai (W), Ecuador (M), Ireland (W), Italy (M), Libya (W, licence), Morocco (M), Philippines (M, W), Singapore (M), Thailand (M), Tunisia (W), Zaire (M), Zambia (M), Zimbabwe-Rhodesia (W).
**Development:** The original SF.260 was a civil three-seat fully aerobatic machine designed by Stelio Frati and flown in 1964. The military M (or MX) series found an immediate market, despite being unnecessarily costly and powerful for a primary trainer and very limited as a combat machine. The three seats, good payload/range at high speed and fully aerobatic capability have made the M series popular, with 138 sold by 1975. Since then the fully armed W (formerly called Warrior) has also found customers, though no sales have been reported of the SW, with increased fuel for 10hr 55min endurance and tip pods housing a camera installation on the right and a Bendix digital radar on the left.

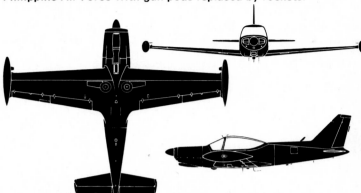

Above: SIAI-Marchetti SF.260WP light attack aircraft of the Philippine Air Force with gun pods replaced by rockets.

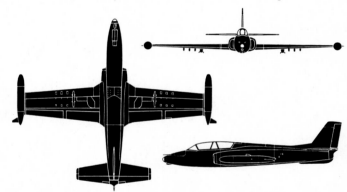

Above: Three-view of SIAI-Marchetti 260M without pylons.

# Soko Galeb and Jastreb

## G2-A, Galeb, J-1 Jastreb

**Origin:** "Soko" Metalopreradivacka Industrija, Yugoslavia.
**Type:** (Galeb) dual armed trainer; Jastreb, single-seat attack.
**Engine:** One Rolls-Royce Viper single-shaft turbojet; (G) 2,500lb (1134kg) thrust Mk 22-6; (J) 3,000lb (1360kg) Mk 531.
**Dimensions:** Span (excluding tip tanks) 34ft 4½in (10·47m); (J) 34ft 8in; length 33ft 11in (10·34m); (J) 35ft 1½in; height 10ft 9in (3·28m); (J) 11ft 11½in.
**Weights:** Empty 5,775lb (2620kg); (J) 6,217lb maximum loaded 9,210lb (4178kg); (G, clean, fully aerobatic) 7,438lb; (J) 10,287lb.
**Performance:** Maximum speed 505mph (812km/h); (J) 510mph; initial climb 4,500ft (1370m)/min; service ceiling 39,375ft (12,000m); range (hi, max fuel) 770 miles (1240km); (J) 945 miles.
**Armament:** (G) 12·7mm guns in nose, each with 80 rounds; underwing pylons for two 220lb (100kg) bombs, or light loads of rockets. (J) three 12·7mm in nose, each with 135 rounds; eight underwing hardpoints, two furthest inboard carrying stores of 551lb (250kg), the rest single 127mm rockets.
**History:** First flight (G) May 1961; service delivery (G) 1965.
**Users:** Libya, Yugoslavia, Zambia.

**Development:** The first Yugoslav jet to go into production, the tandem-seat Galeb (Seagull) has been fully developed and built in modest numbers for the Yugoslav Air Force and Zambia. Pupil and instructor sit in Folland lightweight seats, and an air-conditioning system is an option. The Jastreb (Hawk) uses a similar airframe, with local strengthening for the more powerful engine and heavier external stores. Again Zambia has received an export version, but without the optional cabin pressurization and self-contained engine-start system. Jastrebs can carry cameras in the fuselage and in the nose of the tip tanks, and also tow an aerial target.

Above: Three-view of Soko G2-A Galeb (TJ-1 similar).

Below: The Yugoslav Air Force has about 60 G2-A Galebs, and is receiving a dual trainer/attack model designated TJ-1. About 150 single-seat Jastrebs include the RJ-1 reconnaissance version.

# Soko/CNIAR IAR 93 Orao

## VTI-CIAR 93 Orao

**Origin:** Joint programme by Centrala Industriala Aeronautica Romana, Bucharest, Romania, and Vazduhoplovno-Techniki Institut, Zarkovo, Yugoslavia.

**Type:** Single-seat tactical attack.

**Engines:** Two 4,000lb (1814kg) thrust Rolls-Royce/Fiat Viper 632 single-shaft turbojets.

**Dimensions:** (Estimated) span 24ft 10in (7·56m); length 42ft 4in (12·9m); height 12ft 5in (3·78m).

**Weights:** (Estimated) empty 9,480lb (4300kg); loaded (fighter mission) 15,875lb (7200kg); maximum loaded 19,850lb (9000kg).

**Performance:** (Estimated) maximum speed, equivalent to about Mach 0·95 over wide height band (thus, about 700–720mph, 1150km/h, clean at sea level); maximum speed with weapons, about 550mph (885km/h) at sea level; initial climb (clean) at least 15,000ft (4600m)/min; range on internal fuel (clean, high altitude) about 900 miles (1450km).

**Armament:** Two Nudelmann-Richter NR-30 30mm cannon, each with 125 rounds; centreline and underwing hardpoints, each reported to be rated at 500kg (maximum total external load, 4,840lb, 2200kg) for wide range of Yugoslav cluster bombs, frag bombs, h.e. and napalm (some retarded), rocket pods (12×57mm) or photoflashes.

**History:** Start of design 1971; first flight believed August 1974; official demonstration 15 April 1975; service delivery, probably December 1976.

**Users:** Romania, Yugoslavia.

**Development:** In 1971 the governments of Romania and Yugoslavia agreed to attempt to meet a common requirement of their air forces for a new tactical combat aircraft by building their own. The decision was specifically aimed to help the two countries become more independent of what had previously been a unique source of military equipment. It is significant that the necessary technical help to carry out what was a most challenging project for the two countries came from the West, especially from the UK (which provides engines and most of the airborne system-hardware, and has probably also assisted with the design and development phases). As no bilateral management organization has been announced observers call the project the "Jurom" (Jugoslavia/Romania), but its correct designation is given above (Orao means eagle).

**Above: Three-view of Orao prototype as at first showing in 1975.**

The aircraft is intended to fulfil several important roles, especially tactical interdiction, close-air support (with laser ranger) and multi-sensor reconnaissance. A two-seat version is among the development batch of 11 aircraft, and several of these roles are judged to need a second crew-member (despite the payload/range limitation with aircraft of modest power). The two-seater will also fulfil the need for a trainer more advanced than the Soko Galeb. Later it is hoped to produce a fighter version, with afterburning engines and a lightweight multimode radar. From the start the Orao has been planned to operate from unpaved and relatively short airstrips, though the early pre-production machines did not have the expected slats and double-slotted flaps (but they did have a braking chute and soft-field tyres). By 1977 it was reported that all 11 development aircraft had flown (apparently some assembled in each country, but all bearing the joint VTI-CIAR designation) and that production deliveries were about to begin. If the partners achieve their objective of export sales it may enable work to go ahead on a modern air-combat fighter version with a restressed airframe, and possibly canards, twin vertical tails and double-shock variable inlets. There appears to be the potential in this joint effort for long-term competition for both East and West.

**Below: Prototype Orao landing after making public demonstration at Batajnica airbase near Belgrade on 15 April 1975. Engines are Anglo-Italian, landing gear by Messier-Hispano of France, and many other parts and equipments come from Western Europe or Sweden. Soko of Yugoslavia has project leadership under the VTI, and will assemble about 200; Romania needs about 80.**

# Transall C-160

## C-160D, C-160F and C-160Z

**Origin:** AG Transall, registered in Bremen.
**Type:** Tactical transport.
**Engines:** Two 6,100ehp Rolls-Royce Tyne 22 two-shaft turboprops.
**Dimensions:** Span 131ft 3in (40·00m); length 106ft 3½in (32·40m); height 40ft 6¾in (12·36m).
**Weights:** Empty (equipped) 63,400lb (28,758kg); maximum payload 35,274lb (16,000kg); maximum loaded 112,435lb (51,000kg).
**Performance:** Maximum speed at 16,000ft (4875m) 368mph (592km/h); economical cruise at 20,000ft (6096m) 282mph (454km/h); initial climb 1,300ft (396m)/min; service ceiling 25,500ft (7770m); typical take-off and landing distances over 50ft (15m) with no reverse-pitch on landing 2,900ft (884m); range with max payload and allowances 1,056 miles (1700km); ferry range 3,230 miles (5200km).
**History:** First flight 25 February 1963; service delivery April 1968; last delivery October 1972; start of delivery of additional batch 1979.
**Users:** France (C-160F and civil 160P for Night Mail Service), W Germany (160D), S Africa (160Z) and Turkey (160D).

**Development:** Transall is a name coined from Transporter Allianz, a consortium formed in 1959 by what are today Aérospatiale, MBB and VFW-Fokker. The objective was to produce a military transport to replace the Noratlas (which had been built by both countries) and also meet civil and export needs. Provision was made for jet-lift or jet-boosted STOL versions, but in the event all the 179 production aircraft were basic freighters and the only export sale was nine to S Africa. The engines were made by a consortium (Rolls-Royce, SNECMA, MTU and FN) as were the 18ft (5·5m) propellers (HSD, Rateau-Figeac). The airframe is pressurized and has electric wing and tail anti-icing (almost unique). The 110 bought by the Luftwaffe were more than was needed; 20 were later transferred to Turkey and others are in storage. Despite this in 1976 Aérospatiale secured a commitment from the French government to build a further 75, not to meet customer demand but to maintain employment. The Armée de l'Air has agreed to take 25 of the new batch, and 50 export sales are being sought at a price subsidized to make it competitive.

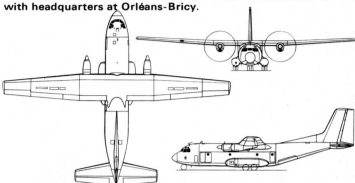

**Above: Takeoff of a C-160F of the 61e Escadre, Armée de l'Air, with headquarters at Orléans-Bricy.**

**Above: Three-view of C-160 (all sub-types similar).**

**Below: A C-160D of the Luftwaffe, which has 76 Transalls in wings LTG 61 and 62 and 14 in an OCU at Wunstorf. Another 20 are in storage, yet Aérospatiale intends to build more.**

# Westland Scout and Wasp

## Scout AH.1 and Wasp HAS.1

**Origin:** See text, production by Westland Helicopters, UK.

**Type:** (S) multi-role tactical helicopter; (W) general utility and ASW helicopter for use from small surface vessels.

**Engine:** (S) one 685shp Rolls-Royce Nimbus 102 free-turbine turboshaft; (WV) 710shp Nimbus 503 (both engines flat-rated from thermodynamic output of 968shp).

**Dimensions:** Diameter of four-blade main rotor 32ft 3in (9·83m); length overall (rotors turning) 40ft 4in (12·29m); length of fuselage 30ft 4in (9·24m); height (rotors turning) 11ft 8in (3·56m).

**Weights:** Empty (S) 3,232lb (1465kg); (W) 3,452lb (1566kg); maximum loaded (S) 5,300lb (2405kg); (W) 5,500lb (2495kg).

**Performance:** Maximum speed at sea level (S) 131mph (211km/h); (W) 120mph (193km/h); maximum (not vertical) rate of climb (S) 1,670ft (510m)/min; (W) 1,440ft (439m)/min; practical manoeuvre ceiling (S) 13,400ft (4085m); (W) 12,200ft (3720m); range with four passengers and reserves (S) 315 miles (510km); (W) 270 miles (435km).

**Armament:** (S) various options including manually aimed guns of up to 20mm calibre, fixed GPMG installations, rocket pods or guided missiles such as SS.11; (W) normally, two Mk 44 torpedoes.

**History:** First flight (P.531) 20 July 1958; (pre-production Scout) 4 August 1960; (production, powered-control AH.1) 6 March 1961; (Wasp HAS.1) 28 October 1962; final delivery (Wasp) 1974.

**Users:** Australia, Bahrein, Brazil, Jordan, New Zealand, Netherlands, S Africa, Uganda, UK (Royal Navy, Army).

**Development:** Designed and originally developed by Saunders-Roe at Eastleigh, these neat helicopters were transferred to Hayes (the former Fairey works) on the merger with Westland and finally all helicopter work was concentrated at Yeovil. Westland built over 100 Scouts for the Army Air Corps, which has used them for every tactical purpose except heavy transport; small numbers were exported to overseas air forces, police, and even the Royal Australian Navy. The more specialised Wasp is used for liaison, ice reconnaissance, search/rescue and many other duties, but its basic task is ASW strike, operating from small destroyer or frigate platforms. Again well over 100 Wasps were built, and about 40 were exported.

**Above: A blue-headed AS.11 anti-tank missile blasts from its launcher on a British Army Scout AH.1 resting on its skids.**

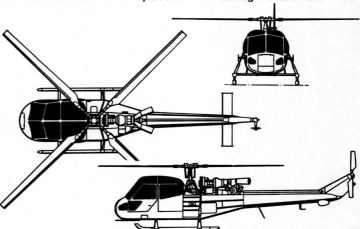

**Above: Three-view of Scout (no weapon pylons or sight).**

**Below: Another blue warhead, this time on a bigger AS.12 fired in the anti-ship role by a Royal Navy Wasp HAS.1.**

# Westland Sea King and Commando

## Sea King HAS.1 and Mks 41-50; Commando 1 and 2

**Origin:** Westland Helicopters, Yeovil, UK (licence from Sikorsky).

**Type:** (Sea King) either anti-submarine or search/rescue transport helicopter; (Commando) tactical helicopter for land warfare.

**Engines:** Two Rolls-Royce Gnome (derived from GE T58) free-turbine turboshaft; past production, mostly 1,500shp Gnome H.1400; current, 1,590shp H.1400-1; future, 1,795shp H.1400-3.

**Dimensions:** Diameter of five-blade main rotor 62ft (18·9m); length overall (rotors turning) 72ft 8in (22·15m); length of fuselage 55ft 10in (17·02m); height (rotors turning) 16ft 10in (5·13m).

**Weights:** Empty (Sea King ASW) 15,474lb (7019kg); (Commando) 12,222lb (5543kg); maximum loaded (H.1400-1 engines) 21,000lb (9525kg).

▶

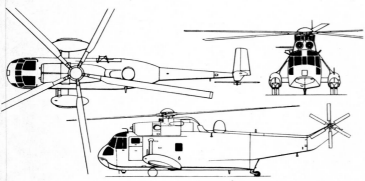

**Above: Three-view of Sea King (Commando differs significantly).**

**Above: Though its airframe is generally similar to that of the Sea King, the Commando is a totally different helicopter for land warfare. Here the simple fixed landing gears are prominent. This design change, and removal of the comprehensive ASW or SAR equipment carried by the Sea King, enables the Commando to carry 28 equipped troops and a wide range of air/surface weapons.**

1 Main rotor blades, incorporating pressurized nitrogen BIM (blade inspection method)
2 Stainless-steel leading-edge strips
3 Blade root fittings
4 Rotor head cowling
5 Fully-articulated main rotor head
6 Cooling grilles
7 Main transmission
8 Access panels
9 Utility reservoir
10 Fire extinguishers
11 Generator
12 Accessories housing
13 Firewall
14 Handhold
15 Turbine exhaust
16 Hinged engine access panel/ work platform
17 Rolls-Royce Gnome 1400-1 turboshaft engine 1,590 hp
18 Pitot heads
19 Turbine intakes
20 Cabin glazing
21 Overhead instrument console
22 Pilot's side window (jettisonable)
23 Co-pilot's (training) seat
24 Pilot's seat
25 Electrically de-iced windscreen
26 Screen washer/wipers
27 Nose access hatch
28 Battery compartment
29 Instrument panel shroud
30 Directional control pedals
31 Side console
32 Fixed landing lights
33 Forward electronics bay
34 Electronics bay handle
35 Adjustable landing light
36 Nose beacon
37 Underfloor avionics bay
38 Navigation systems (Dopper/ADF/VOR)
39 Automatic flight control system
40 Cockpit/cabin bulkhead
41 Commander's folding jump seat
42 Starboard cabin window/ escape hatch
43 Port entry door (lower half with integral steps)
44 Port entry door (upper half)
45 Engine/cabin firewall bulkhead
46 Strut/fuselage attachment fairing
47 Foothold
48 Door rail (starboard)
49 Fixed strut (emergency energy-absorbing)
50 Fuselage frame
51 Fuselage structure
52 Starboard sliding cargo door
53 Port missile shoe (optional)
54 Port cabin window/escape hatch
55 Door-mounted machine-gun (starboard)
56 Inflatable rubberized nylon troop seats (26)
57 Auxiliary internal fuel tanks
58 Fuselage stringers
59 Aft fixed window
60 Aft cabin bulkhead
61 UHF aerial
62 Spine shaft housing
63 Transmission shaft
64 Tailboom L-section stringers
65 Intermediate gearbox
66 Fixed tailplane (starboard)
67 Tail-rotor transmission shaft
68 Anti-collision beacon
69 Six-blade aluminium-alloy rotor
70 Hub spider
71 Rail rotor stub
72 Fixed tail pylon
73 Glass-fibre access panels
74 Cable/push-rod transition quadrant
75 Tailboom skinning
76 Tailboom frames
77 Tailwheel mounting
78 Aft keel frame
79 Tailwheel shock-absorber
80 Fixed tailwheel
81 Fuel jettison pipe
82 Aerial
83 Fuel system aft bay
84 Underfloor bulkhead
85 Cargo floor (tie-down points)
86 Ventral skinning
87 Undercarriage fixed sponson
88 Mainwheel leg fairing
89 Cargo sling frame
90 Mainwheel shock-absorbers
91 Port twin mainwheels
92 Personnel rescue hoist (winch above starboard cargo door)
93 Cargo sling
94 Sling wires
95 Port Minigun pòd
96 Multi-barrel muzzle shroud
97 Fuel-system forward bay
98 Starboard gun pod
99 Muzzle shroud
100 Anti-collision beacon
101 Missile shoe
102 Starboard ASM (optional provision)
103 Starboard mainwheel leg fairing
104 Oleo shock absorbers
105 Starboard mainwheels

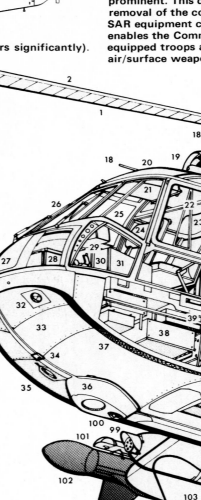

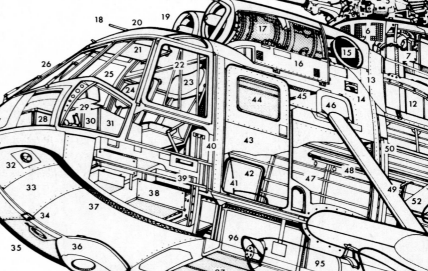

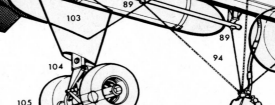

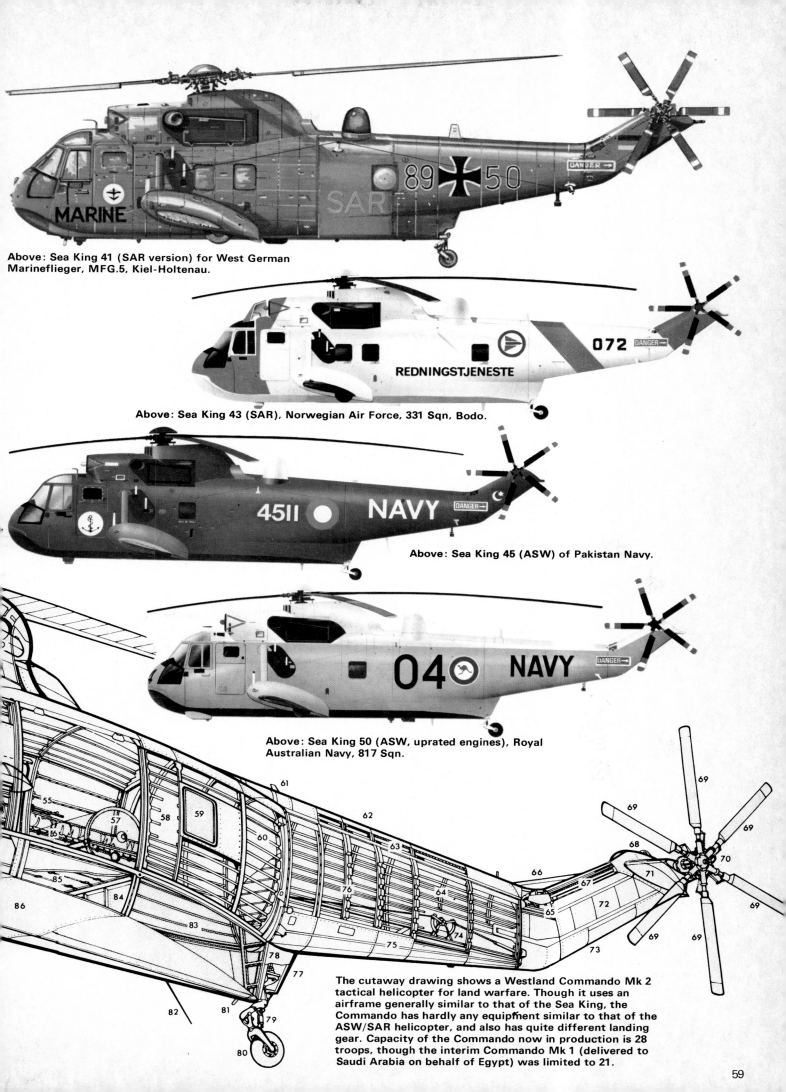

Above: Sea King 41 (SAR version) for West German Marineflieger, MFG.5, Kiel-Holtenau.

Above: Sea King 43 (SAR), Norwegian Air Force, 331 Sqn, Bodo.

Above: Sea King 45 (ASW) of Pakistan Navy.

Above: Sea King 50 (ASW, uprated engines), Royal Australian Navy, 817 Sqn.

The cutaway drawing shows a Westland Commando Mk 2 tactical helicopter for land warfare. Though it uses an airframe generally similar to that of the Sea King, the Commando has hardly any equipment similar to that of the ASW/SAR helicopter, and also has quite different landing gear. Capacity of the Commando now in production is 28 troops, though the interim Commando Mk 1 (delivered to Saudi Arabia on behalf of Egypt) was limited to 21.

**Performance:** Maximum speed 143mph (230km/h); typical cruising speed 131mph (211km/h); maximum (not vertical) rate of climb (ASW) 1,770ft (540m)/min; (Commando) 2,020ft (616m)/min; approved ceiling 10,000ft (3048m); range (maximum load) about 350 miles (563km), (maximum fuel) 937 miles (1507km).
**Armament:** See text.
**History:** Derived from Sikorsky S-61 of 1959; first flight of Sea King 7 May 1969; (Commando) September 1973.
**Users:** Australia; Belgium, Egypt, W Germany, India, Norway, Pakistan, Qatar, Saudi Arabia, UK (RAF, Royal Navy).

**Development:** Sikorsky's S-61 was almost inevitably the subject of a licence agreement between the company and Westland Aircraft, continuing an association begun in 1947 when a licence was purchased to make the S-51. In the case of the S-61 the most immediate significant customer was the Royal Navy, which was searching for an ASW (anti-submarine warfare) helicopter to supplement and eventually replace the Wessex in operation from surface ships. Unlike the US Navy, which chose to regard its ASW helicopters as mere extensions of the all-important ship, the Fleet Air Arm concluded it would be preferable to allow the helicopter to operate independently. The Sea King HAS.1 was thus designed to carry sensors, weapons and a complete tactical centre to hunt down and destroy submerged submarines. The normal equipment for Sea Kings in the ASW role includes dunking sonar, doppler navigator, search radar and an auto-pilot and weapon system providing for automatic hovering at given heights or for a range of other automatic manoeuvres in all weather. The RN bought 56, with 13 more ordered in 1975 and eight in 1976. Total Sea King sales are close to 150, many of them being for the much simpler SAR (search and rescue) version with seats for up to 22, apart from the crew, and special provision for casualties, cargo and slung loads. The future RAF rescue helicopter is the Sea King HAR. 3.

Likely to find as large a market during the coming decade, the Commando is a purely land-based aircraft with fixed landing gear devoid of floats. It has been optimised to the range/payload needs of tactical operations, and carries much special equipment for use in a wide range of roles. The basic Commando provides accommodation for up to 28 troops in the transport role, or equivalent cargo payload (or 8,000lb, 3630kg, slung externally). Other roles include logistic support, casualty evacuation, search/rescue or, with any of a wide range of armament fits, air/surface strike. So far no armed Commandos have been ordered (the first sale was a large batch for Egypt, bought by Saudi Arabia in 1973), but various turrets and launchers, manually aimed guns, guided missiles and rocket pods can be fitted. Internal load can include a 105mm gun or Shorland armoured car.

**Above: A Royal Navy Sea King HAS.1 dunks its Plessey Type 195 sonar to listen for submarines. Note the twin depressions caused by the split rotor downwash (not heard by the sonar).**

# Westland/Aérospatiale Lynx

## Lynx AH.1, HAS.2 and 2(FN) and HT.3.

**Origin:** Westland Helicopters, UK, in partnership with Aérospatiale, France.
**Type:** Multi-role helicopter (see text).
**Engines:** Two 900shp Rolls-Royce Gem 10001 three-shaft turbines; uprated aircraft, 1,050shp Gem 4.
**Dimensions:** Diameter of four-blade main rotor 42ft (12·80m); length overall (rotors turning) 49ft 9in (15·16m); height overall (rotors turning) 12ft (3·66m).
**Weights:** Empty weight (basic) 5,225lb (2370kg); empty (equipped for troop transport) 5,641lb (2558kg), (anti-tank) 6,313lb (2863kg), (dunking sonar search/strike) 7,218lb (3274kg); maximum loaded (army) 9,250lb (4196kg), (navy) 9,500lb (4309kg).
**Performance:** Maximum speed 207mph (333km/h); continuous cruise 176mph (284km/h); single-engine cruise 164mph (263km/h); maximum (not vertical) rate of climb 2,370ft (722m)/min; ceiling, well over 25,000ft (7600m); range (army) 473 miles (761km), (navy) 418 miles (673km); ferry range with cabin tank 861 miles (1386km).
**Armament:** See text.
**History:** First flight 21 March 1971; (HAS.2) 25 May 1972; service delivery (Royal Navy) May 1976.
**Users:** Argentina, Belgium, Brazil, Denmark, Egypt (planned licence-manufacture complete with engine), France (Navy), W Germany (Navy), Netherlands, Norway, Qatar, UK (RAF, Royal Navy, Army).

**Development:** Certain to be manufactured in very large numbers over a period greater than ten years, the Lynx is probably the outstanding example

today of a military multi-role helicopter. Its agility is unsurpassed and its avionics and flight system provide for easy one-man operation in bad weather with minimal workload. Designed by Westland but built in 70/30 partnership with Aérospatiale of France, with contributions from certain other nations, the Lynx is sized to carry ten men (13 in civil versions) and has outstanding performance and smoothness, and early in development was looped, rolled at 100°/sec and flown backwards at 80mph. The AH.1 is tailored to many battlefield duties, can carry almost all available helicopter sight systems, guns and missiles, and is proving a superior tank-killer. The HAS.2, with the Seaspray radar, performs virtually all shipboard roles including anti-submarine classification/strike, vertical replenishment, air/surface search/strike (using Sea Skua missiles), search/rescue, fire support and other duties. In 1979 the Lynx was joined by prototypes of the WG.30 in which the Gem 4 (used in many Lynx) is matched with slightly larger rotors and a dramatically enlarged fuselage with cabin bigger even than that of a Puma, with seats for up to 23. Many military sales of the WG.30 were being discussed in late 1979.

**Above: Three-view of Lynx AH.1 with side view (top) of HAS.2.**

**Facing page, upper: A Lynx HAS.2 of the Royal Navy comes aboard HMS *Sheffield*, first of the Type 42 surface warships. Facing page, lower: Lynx HAS multi-role variant of Royal Netherlands Navy, with Seaspray radar. The final ten Dutch Lynx are fitted with uprated Gem engines and weigh 10,500lb (4763kg).**

**Below: The Lynx is the world's most manoeuvrable combat helo, and it has rolled (like this Army AH.1) at over 100° per second and flown backwards at 80mph.**

**Above: Prototype Lynx HAS.2 with AS.12 (now replaced by Sea Skua).**